Edyta Tadeusiak

HOW TO BUY YOUR FIRST HOUSE IN THE UK

Cover design:
Aneta Pietura

Desktop publishing:
Adrian Szatkowski, zecernia.net

*This book is dedicated to my employees, for their hard work
and commitment – with them, everything became possible.
And to my mentors who taught me to dream, and to bring
my dreams to life. Thank you, every one of you.*

Table of Contents

1. Introduction

If you're reading this book, it probably means you've decided to buy a property in the UK. This book is aimed to empower you with the tools and knowledge of the *'property world'*, so that the property you buy becomes a profitable investment. This book will give you insight of not only where to gather all the information needed when purchasing a property; but also provide you with a breadth of information ranging from architect's advice to individuals' property investment journey.

If you've just begun to think about buying a property, this book is for you. By the end of this book you will be filled with confidence and knowledge to make future investments. Property investments can be very profitable, and more important, they also offer unlimited possibilities to hone new skills. If you've been thinking about buying for quite some time, now is the opportunity to turn that 'thought' into an investment. In most cases buying in the UK is very different from what it looks elsewhere – in the UK, people typically change the place of their residence several times within their lifetime. This can be down to various factors around family, study or financial situation; although the attitude of many people towards buying a property is usually geared around making money from it. It's likely to be the most expensive purchase that you may encounter, making it extremely difficult for some people to achieve this goal. In this context it's good to remember Robert Kiyosaki's words:

«I can't afford it» shuts down your brain.

To change that mindset, he suggests to say…

«How can I afford it?» opened up the brain.

Allowing you to think and search for answers, opening up the possibility to achieve that goal.

Buying a property in the UK brings a lot of benefits of home ownership, both financial and non-financial. This book offers an overview of the whole buying process and familiarises you with relevant rules and regulations, so that you feel well prepared to take the first step. It'll also identify potential risks that you should be wary of when making investment decisions. After all, it's easy to oversee the risks when you're excited over a purchase. The most important principle you should bear in mind is that you earn money by buying a property and not by selling it. If you don't have time for buying, get somebody to do it for you for a fee – this can save you a lot of money. John Paul Getty once said: *"I would rather earn 1% off a 100 people's efforts than 100% of my own efforts"*. You can read more about it further on in this book.

First-time buyers are frequently targeted by political parties. In effect, they seem a privileged group that the British government provides multiple help initiatives to get on the property market. In the following chapters I'll explain how you could utilise the governments help when buying a property. You'll also be provided with information on how the government could help if you lost your job, or if you struggled with mortgage repayments.

Buying a house is a goal that the majority of people would love to achieve as soon as possible. I believe it's better to go through this process slowly and consciously, learning about and getting to understand its different aspects, so that, eventually we can also encourage and help others. It's worth sharing your plans of buying a property with other people, especially those whom you look up to and respect. This helps to stay focused on making your plan a reality.

Many people who may have come to the UK for work and/or study resign from buying their own house, only because they don't plan to stay in the UK indefinitely. The question is why shouldn't they? There is, and always will be, a huge demand for rental properties in the UK. If you decide to leave the country, you can always change the type of mortgage that you have from residential to buy-to-let. Your interest rate will be slightly higher, but the mortgage can change from repaying the capital to interest only, so your monthly repayment should be a lot lower (remember that for this type of mortgage, your deposit must be around 20–25%). The rent from letting out your house will surely cover the monthly repayment, insurance and management fee. In most cases there'll also be a small sum left. What's more, the value of your house will be steadily growing – for the last 60 years, the value of properties in the UK has been increasing year on year. If there's a property market crash, you should remember that crisis fuels change and improves the quality of life. As Warren Buffett said – if you don't find a way to make money while you sleep, you will work until you die. The hope is that this book will influence your outlook on property investment's and give you the courage to take the plunge.

Let's begin!

2. Property Journey

My property journey began with the purchase of my first property in the UK around January 2006, just two and a half years after I came into the country. I'll never forget the day when I collected the keys. The cost of the flat was £183,000 and my deposit was £18,300 plus all the fees and stamp duty totalled to roughly £22,000. But my property journey wasn't straight forward, as the only savings that I had available was £16,000 which wasn't sufficient to purchase the property. My friend, Edyta (to whom I'll always be grateful) lent me £4000, and I withdrew £2000 from my credit card to assist in acquiring all the funds.

There wasn't anyone that I knew who could give me any practical guidance – all my friends were renting, therefore unable to give advice on buying a property. I arranged a mortgage appointment at NatWest bank, just because a member of staff there had a Polish-sounding name on his name badge. Unfortunately, I was informed that I didn't earn enough to get a mortgage. Besides, being a waitress, I was perceived as an unreliable client by the bank. In order to move forward, I had to put a lot of thought into the next stages in resolving how to get on the 'property ladder'. For over three months I worked 14 hour long days. My employer wrote a letter of recommendation for me, confirming that I was assisting a manager. This then assisted into obtaining a mortgage, and three months later I could buy my first three-bedroom dream flat in Wood Green.

Swiftly, I realised that property buying was a simple way to achieve financial independence. And, immediately I decided to earn money for another property. To speed this process up, I let out the rooms in the newly bought property. Fourteen months on, and I accumulated enough capital to buy a second property but, this time, the process of buying was more straightforward as I was buying with my partner. It allowed for a greater choice of properties, as the mortgage was given on a dual income basis and combined we had a larger deposit. This time a decision was granted within three weeks from the lender Abbey (now

Santander). We decided that it was to be a house, ideally with a big garden, and potential for it to be turned into something spectacular – to this we found the perfect two bedroom house with lots of potential.

Before moving forward with the second property, I had to change the first from a residential to a buy to let (BTL) mortgage, so my broker applied to NatWest, who at the time had the best deal. The property increased in value enough to allow me to get the mortgage for the original amount borrowed. *Note: Currently, you would need to have 15–25% deposit to be able to get buy to let mortgage.* The good news was, the mortgage repayment changed to interest only, therefore the amount decreased from roughly £900 to £550 per month. This simply meant that I was now able to save enough for a third property even quicker than expected. After four months of work on the second property, it was transformed into a 3 bedrooms, 2 receptions with kitchen dinner and 2 bathrooms. A year on, we converted the loft space into a large bedroom with an ensuite bathroom. Ten years' later the property was valued at 130% more than the original value.

🔔 **Remember!**

If you sell your residential property, that you lived in and didn't let out or used it for business purposes, you do not need to pay capital gains tax. You will automatically get a tax relief called Private Residence Relief. For any property that isn't your main home, such as BTL or businesses premises, then you will be subjected to tax. For more information and working out your tax go to www.gov.uk/capital-gains-tax

---

Buying your first or second property does not have to end there, you can consider investing in a holiday home in UK or abroad. For me, I ventured to Spain continuing my property journey. My experience, as well as countless other people's property journey and expertise detailed in this book, prove that you can always find a way to achieve what you desire, you just need to be prepared for the challenges ahead and take one step at a time. In order to succeed, you must define your strategy, set the goals and time frame. If you don't have money for a deposit, you need to be creative. There are many areas in which you can explore such as; finding another job, selling unwanted possessions on eBay, putting an ad on a website or newspaper saying that you can become somebody's virtual assistant after your working hours, let out a room or two in a flat or a house that you are renting (if the owner agrees for subletting). HMRC allows home-owners or home-occupiers to earn a certain amount of tax-free income from letting out furnished rooms in their home. Make the lack of cash inspire you.

As the motivational speaker Jacek Walkiewicz says – ...every excuse, even one that's really good, has one aim: to excuse our lack of action and to make us feel better. The guilt we feel because of procrastination is a very convenient way of escape. We focus on what we can't do instead of using the possibilities to succeed. Fulfil your plans, act with passion and enjoy the outcomes. Remember that a bad decision is better than no decision. The secret to life satisfaction is the personal effort that we put into the things that we desire – this however is a very individual experience and can mean different things to different people. All that comes easy also goes easy and is easily forgotten. Professor Bartoszewski encouraged his audience to live a life that may not necessarily be easy, but one that at least isn't boring.

3. Why is it better to buy than to rent?

Buying a property can be your first step towards generating profits from real estate. As soon as you buy a house, you start saving. First, you stop paying rent. Then, if you refurbish or modernise your home, you increase its market value. What's more, when you buy a property with the help of a mortgage loan, usually monthly mortgage repayments are lower than the rent you pay while renting a house. So, thanks to your investment, you start saving money.

Here are the benefits that you could have with property investment in the UK:

1. You make the first step towards financial freedom – you begin accumulating passive income, which will let you decide how to invest your time.
2. Money which you've paid into your deposit (5–10% of the property price) is a good investment.
3. If you decide to let out part of your home, or even a whole house in the future, you will gain additional income that won't require too much of your time or effort.
4. The investment protects you against inflation.
5. The property investment is low-risk in comparison to opening a business, which usually requires a lot of financial involvement and doesn't guarantee success.

Summary of the chapter:
1. It's better to buy a property rather than rent it.
2. Buying offers several financial benefits.
3. You can prepare yourself for buying (do the exercise below).

Everybody is different. Some of us are afraid of failure, some of us are afraid of success. Write down your concerns and worries regarding buying a property. Next, try to challenge them, using examples from your own life. Jot down your thoughts next to each of the statements you've written previously.

4. Different types of properties in the United Kingdom

There're different forms of property ownership and different types of residential housing in the UK. Try to remain open to different possibilities and think in terms of the value for money property. Sometimes it's not worth paying £300,000 for a two-bedroom house with a garden, if you could have a two-bedroom flat with a garden in the same location for £200,000. Monthly repayment for a property worth £100,000 less will be one-third lower. You must ask yourself whether this will be your home for a few years, or longer.

There're the following types of **residential housing** in the UK:

– detached and semi-detached single family houses (for example cottages, bungalows and mansions etc.)
– single-family terraced houses
– blocks of flats

Popular **types of houses** available in the UK:

1. *End of terrace* – the first or the last house in a row of attached houses, which share side walls. Because you share only one wall with your neighbours, these houses tend to be 10% more expensive than the houses in the middle of a row. It's worth checking how big the garden is, or what the non-attached side of the house looks like, and whether it's possible to build an extension.

2. *Mid-terraced* – a house in the middle of a row of attached houses sharing both side walls with neighbours. This type of housing is usually slightly cheaper, but this comes with a price tag. One disadvantage is the fact that in older properties there's no good acoustic isolation, so if you have loud neighbours, this could be a problem. On the other hand, these houses are warmer, especially in winter, therefore requiring you to pay less for heating.

3. ***Detached (and semi-detached)*** – a free-standing house (or one of the two separate houses sharing a common wall) usually worth 20–25% more than a terraced property, as they offer more space and privacy.
4. ***Bungalow*** – a one-level house built specially for people with mobility issues (older or disabled people). They tend to cost more, are more spacious, and have a large garden.
5. ***Maisonette*** – usually a two-level split flat with private entrance. Frequently located above commercial properties, it can also be an extension to a regular house. Sometimes the entrance of the maisonette can be located at the rear side of the building and/or lead through the fire escape.
6. ***Purpose-built flat*** – a flat in a typical block of flats with shared communal space (for example, a staircase). It has been constructed from the beginning as a flat, rather than being converted.

Single-family houses are mostly sold with a piece of land they've been built on, whereas apartments in a block of flats belong mostly to the owner of the land (the freeholder). The flats are then sold as a leasehold and the buyers have the right to occupy the property for as long as the lease is valid.

Forms of **legal ownership** of a property:
1. ***Freehold*** – you're buying a property together with the piece of land, on which it's located (or with a share in the ownership rights to this land, if the purchase concerns a flat that's part of a dwelling house). After completing the purchase, the lawyer will register your details in the land registry. If you have a mortgage, the bank will have a first charge over the property in the land registry. This means that when you sell your property, the bank will be the first to receive its money. You are, however, the owner of the "title absolute" in the land registry.
2. ***Leasehold*** – almost all flats and apartments are leasehold. This means that you own the property (for the amount of years specified in your leasehold contract) but rent the land on which it's built. The lease is usually long and can last from 90 to 125 years, sometimes even 999 years – this is the so-called

'peppercorn'. A freeholder is responsible for common areas of the building, such as a staircase, external walls, roof, etc. A leaseholder is obliged to pay service charge, which includes building maintenance fees, replacement of bulbs, sometimes cleaning of the communal area, servicing elevators, staircase lighting, building insurance, as well as the ground rent. Those costs in London are usually around £100 per month, whereas in luxury apartments it can be even around £4000 per year.

It's worth checking how high those costs are before making an offer. Sometimes, especially if it only concerns a house consisting of two apartments, the fee is only about £250 per year and covers only renting of the land (ground rent). After the agreed lease period expires, for example after 90 years, you may have the option to buy the land and become the freeholder yourself or, more commonly, to extend your lease. In fact, you can extend at any time before that, and the earlier you do it, the cheaper it usually is. If, however, the lease expires and you don't extend it, the ownership goes back to the freeholder.

You should check, if/when extending the lease would be possible and ask for the renewal cost. If the lease period for a flat is less than 80 years, it's much more difficult to get a mortgage. In this situation you can request a quote for lease extension. Remember that if the remaining lease falls below 80 years, the costs of the lease extension are drastically increasing ('80 year' rule). Therefore, it's much better to apply for lease extension when you still have 81 years of lease rather than 79 years. The difference in cost is immense.

3. *Share of freehold* – in some cases instead of leasehold, a share of freehold is offered. Instead of renting the land on which the property is located, the owner (freeholder), sells it. In other words, what's being sold is the right of separate ownership of the premises together with a share in the communal area of the building, and in the joint ownership of the land. The owners of the premises are then jointly responsible for all repairs, building insurance and management of communal areas. As mentioned earlier, these include the staircase, the external wall, and the roof.

Summary of the chapter:

1. There're many different types of property ownership in the UK. Get to know them all.
2. There're also many different types of residential housing – check which one will be most suitable for you.
3. Remember that you should choose the property that will give you the best earning opportunities.

Your subconscious mind knows no difference between what's really happened and what you've seen in your imagination. That's why visualisation is a very important motivational technique. Starting from today, spend a few minutes each day imagining that you've achieved your goal. Think about the smallest details – how you feel, how you look, how other people treat you. If your goal is purchase of a property – what does it look like, what are the circumstances of signing the purchase contract and receiving keys, etc.

5. Mortgage

If you're going to invest in properties, it's worth learning basic terminology first. The whole process will then become less scary and intimidating.

Mortgage is a loan which you get from the lender (banks or building societies) and that is secured against the property you're buying. In other words, the lender is a co-owner of your house until you repay your mortgage. If you decide to sell your property, the money from this transaction goes to the lender first. The rest covers the fees of a solicitor or a licensed conveyancer; depending on the amount of equity in the property, the remaining will be deposited to you.

🔔 Remember!

Many people think that one of the criteria of getting a mortgage in the UK is having British citizenship or a settled status. If you're an EU citizen, you can get a mortgage if you have lived in the UK for at least three years, have a UK bank account and a permanent job. If you were born outside of the UK and EU, you should have permanent residency or indefinite leave to remain, you must have been a resident in the UK for more than two years, and you need a UK bank account, a permanent job in the UK and a deposit of at least 25%.

Building Societies are bodies which operate in the UK housing market. Several decades ago Building Societies played a major role as lenders for property buying in the UK. Building Societies collect deposits from buyers and give mortgage loans. Banks and building societies like lending money in this way since the risk is minimal. This is because firstly, the mortgage is secured against the property value, and secondly, you're obliged to buy a building insurance that will protect you and the bank against fire, flood and the problems with the building's structure.

Mortgage affordability

It all depends on a given bank's policy. Usually the mortgage is four to five times your annual income. Also, a very important factor is your own financial contribution – if your deposit is only 5% of a property's value, it's very probable that your mortgage will be higher than it would be with the deposit of 10% or 15%. The banks can also consider how many people you support. Additionally they will take into account any regular financial commitments you might have, e.g. personal loans, car finance, credit cards, school fees, etc.

📖 **Example**

If you earn around £25,000 a year, most probably you'll be able to borrow around £112,000. So, if you have savings of £10,000 (your deposit), you will be looking for a house for around £122,000 (mortgage of £112,000 plus your savings of £10,000 sum up to £122,000). However, this amount may be reduced due to your financial obligations in the form of loans, credit accounts and the number of dependants.

Mortgages and repayment methods

Repayment mortgage – repayment of the loan with interest according to the schedule set by the lender. If you have a loan for 20 years, the repayment instalments with interest will be combined so that you repay the loan and interest due within a specified period. There are different types of interest rates for repayment mortgages: fixed-rate, flexible-rate and variable-rate.

Fixed rate mortgage – the bank schedules monthly repayments of interest and capital in the form of fixed mortgage instalments usually for two, three or five years. Regardless of the Bank of England base rate and the existing market circumstances, the monthly repayment is the same throughout the set period. After the expiration of this period you can ask for the repayments to remain fixed. You will be then offered a possibility of remortgaging (with the current or another bank).

This repayment method resembles paying the rent when renting out a dwelling – you pay the same amount over the period you have committed to by signing a contract with the bank. If you decided to sell the property before the term ends or change to a different bank, it may result in a penalty known as Early Repayment Charge (ERC). For most of the banks, the fee ranges from 1% to 3% of the loan value. Some banks have fixed costs, while others don't charge anything. While applying for a mortgage, check those additional costs with your bank.

Variable interest rate mortgage – monthly repayment may fluctuate due to being tied to the change of interest rates of the central bank (the Bank of England base rate) and the standard variable rate of a given bank. The most common types of mortgages with variable interest rates are a tracker mortgage (depending on the Bank of England base rate) and a discount mortgage (related to the base interest rate of a given lender).

In June 2019 the Bank of England base rate was 0.75%, at the moment, in September 2020, due to COVID-19 it is 0.1%, lowest in history. Therefore, I don't recommend this option – it may turn out risky, as the interest rates will most likely be raised soon. The advantage of this type of mortgages may be that they often offer the possibility of unlimited overpayments or of an early repayment. This option may be right for people intending to sell their property or planning a move in the short run.

Flexible mortgage – this solution is intended for people who work as self-employed or for a commission, and whose earnings are different every month. This form of repayment is not very popular and banks dislike it. They may, usually offer a reduction in the number of years of mortgage, rather than a reduction of the monthly amount. However, you can pay in more than your monthly instalment and this fund will be used when you need it. Flexible mortgages are available with fixed or variable interest rates. Personally, I'd recommend a flexible fixed rate mortgage because you always know your monthly repayment.

Capped mortgage – a type of a loan with a variable interest rate. Monthly interest payments fluctuate, depending on changes of the standard variable rate, but cannot exceed the highest value set. You can apply for a capped mortgage individually or jointly with other people.

Offset mortgage – a combination of a loan and a savings account. Thanks to the savings you have on a special savings account the bank reduces how much interest you're being charged.

Joint mortgage – a loan that you take on with another person: a partner, a friend or a roommate. Together you have a higher deposit and higher income, and you can get a bigger mortgage and a lower interest rate.

Some lenders offer the option of jointly applying for a mortgage even by 4 people. In this way the lender can base their mortgage offer on the joint income of all the applicants, which can translate into a higher loan.

The following **types of ownership** are possible when considering a joint mortgage:

- **Joint tenants** – sometimes also referred to as "beneficial joint tenants"; – buyers have equal ownership rights to the property. If one of the owners dies, the ownership right automatically goes to the co-owner. You cannot bequeath your part of the property to someone else in your will.
- **Tenants in common** – you can have any percentage of shares, usually depending on how much financial contribution you bring in. In the event of your death the property doesn't automatically become the property of the people you bought it with, and you can bequeath your shares in the will to whoever you want.

If you decide to buy a property for letting, you can take out an investment property loan (buy-to-let mortgage – BTL), which is completely different from your first mortgage. To get it on favourable terms, you must be the owner of the house where you live – regardless if it was bought for cash or through mortgage.

The most common requirements for BTL mortgage are as follows:
- Your expenses don't exceed your earnings and you have a good credit history;
- You earn at least £25,000 a year (if two people are buying, the sum of the required earnings is usually £30,000, which also means that one person can earn more than £30,000 and the other can earn less);
- The rent associated with a given property should be at least 25% higher than a monthly mortgage repayment.

Nowadays, when granting BTL mortgages, banks apply the so-called stress test. They determine the projected interest rate of the loan at 5.5%. When applying for BTL worth £100,000, its annual interest will be £5,500. That is why the rent must be 125% of this amount. In this case, this would be at least £575 per month. If the property is classed as non-standard, the lender can require a 40% deposit for security. The bigger the deposit, the lower the interest rate. Almost all BTL mortgages are interest-only, which means that you only pay the interest. Your monthly repayments are much lower, but you must have an investment plan or repayment strategy to pay off the mortgage in the future, for example in 25 years' time.

Mortgage for students

Student mortgages are becoming a popular method for stepping onto the property ladder for first time buyers. With the increasing rise in costs of student and rental accommodation, both parents and students are realising that this a more profitable way to pay for accommodation as well as obtaining a property at the end of it. This type of mortgage does not require the borrower and guarantor to deposit any money upfront in order to secure the mortgage; instead the lender puts a charge against the guarantor(s) home to cover any risks. The student (borrower) will need to keep up with the monthly payments as the guarantor(s) will then be responsible for the loan. In my personal and professional opinion it is a remarkable option, one that not many people know exists. What's more, this could be used as an investment by renting out any additional bedrooms to other students which will assist in covering the mortgage payments. The mortgage will be interest only making the repayments relatively low.

'Buy for uni' Q&A Session: Mortgage Adviser

1. Are there any mortgages available for students?
- Good news for students; there are two banks currently offering "buy for uni" mortgages. Students can borrow up to 100% of the property value.
- They don't need to have a deposit.
- The student does not have to pay tax on the rental income or the higher stamp duty that landlords normally have to pay when buying a second home because they can use their personal income tax allowance and rent a room relief.
- If they are first time buyers; the house purchased by the student is treated as the student's main residence, so there is a lower or no stamp duty. There is no capital gains tax on sales.

📖 Example

If you wanted to buy a three bedroom property for £140,000 and have parents (guarantors) that has a house valued at £550,000. The bank or building society will put a charge of £35,000 against your guarantor's property, and then lend the borrower £140,000 for their property that they wish to purchase.

An interest only mortgage for a property such as this costs on average £580 per month on a 5% interest rate. In 2020 the average student accommodation costs per person is £547 per month (outside of London). With, an additional two spare rooms that could be rented out, the mortgage will be covered along with additional costs leaving the student (landlord) rent free and with an investment at the end of their studies.

2. **What are the advantages of this type of mortgage and why is it better than renting?**
   – Payback tend to be more manageable and affordable.
   – Quicker way to get on the property ladder.
   – Many of the students who took advantage of this loan were able to make a significant profit over the 4 years of study. This allowed some of them to buy an apartment outside of London for cash, without a mortgage. In my opinion, renting is a waste of money.

3. **Who pays the mortgage and are there any restrictions?**
   – The mortgage can be covered by rent from letting out additional rooms in the property.
   – Buyers are restricted to three-bedroom homes, no HMOs allowed.
   – Maximum loan size of £300,000 to £400,000.
   – The main guarantor must have a sustainable income.

4. Does the guarantor have to remain on the agreement until the mortgage is paid off?

– It doesn't have to be a continuous arrangement for the guarantor – if there comes a time when the borrower can make the repayments themselves they can apply to have the guarantor(s) released from the agreement (subject to affordability checks and evidence).

5. What are the eligibility criteria?

– If the student has a form of employed or self-employed income, they can purchase the property however may still need a guarantor.
– The guarantor must be a direct family member or legal guardian who owns a property.
– They must live in the UK and have permanent residency rights.
– Maximum age of guarantor must not be over 65 years of age.

Contribution by Robert Bieniasz, contact details below:

Robert Bieniasz

Mortgage Adviser
T&L Centre
m: 079 5827 8101

As a first-time buyer applying for a mortgage, you're currently exempt from paying the stamp duty land tax (SDLT). In 2017 Chancellor of the Exchequer, Philip Hammond, announced an increase in the threshold from which to apply for a stamp duty exemption when buying a property. All first-time buyers in England, Wales and Northern Ireland buying a house worth up to £300,000 will not pay any tax for the purchase of their first property. Before 22nd of November 2017 the buyers purchasing a property worth £300,000 had to pay a tax rate of £5000.

First-time buyers who purchase a property worth between £300,000–£500,000 also benefit from the change in law. In this case, the tax will only be charged on the amount over the threshold value of £300,000. The standard rates apply only to people who have previously owned a residential property, or who are buying a property worth more than £500,000. Remember that if you're, or have previously been, the owner of a property anywhere else in the world, you will lose the status of the first-time buyer and the privileges described above.

If you buy a property for letting out, you need to pay the stamp duty tax. The tax amount will be based on the value of the property according to the scale presented below:

Buy-to-let Stamp Duty tax when you already have one property and you're buying another property		
Minimal property value	Maximal property value	STAMP DUTY RATE
£0	£125,000	3%
£125,001	£250,000	5%
£250,001	£925,000	8%
£925,001	£1,5 m	13%
More than £1,5 m		15%

Stamp Duty Rate – First Time Buyer for properties worth less than £500,000		
Minimal property value	Maximal property value	STAMP DUTY RATE
£0	£300,000	0%
£300,001	£500,000	5%
£500,001	£925,000	5%
£925,001	£1,5 m	8%
More than £1,5 m		12%

Sample calculations **House price £450,000**
– The first £300,000 is exempt from Stamp Duty tax.
– The remaining £150,000 is taxed at 5% of Stamp Duty rate.
– Amount to pay £7,500.

Stamp Duty Rate – First Time Buyer for properties worth more than £500,000		
Minimal property value	**Maximal property value**	**STAMP DUTY RATE**
£0	£125,000	0%
£125,001	£250,000	2%
£250,001	£925,000	5%
£925,001	£1,5 m	10%
More than £1,5 m		12%

Sample calculations **House price £675,000**
- The first £125,000 is exempt from Stamp Duty tax.
- The following £125,000 is charged a 2% Stamp Duty tax – £2500
- The rest of the amount, £425,000 is charged a 5% Stamp Duty tax – £21,250,000
- All in all, the Stamp Duty tax amounts to £23,750

Understanding deposits

The deposit is your own financial contribution towards the purchase of the property. This can be your savings, a gift from a family member or, in some cases, a loan from the bank, or money taken from the credit card. However, this is unsecured credit and it will reduce the overall amount that the mortgage lender will offer. In practice, banks don't like it when the money for the deposit comes from a loan, especially a bank loan, but a lot of people buy their first property in this way. During the mortgage application process the bank will ask you where the money for the deposit comes from. You must document all the funds with appropriate paperwork, so it's worth preparing for this well in advance.

Ask yourself, how much you'd be able to pay off monthly. I strongly encourage you to look at additional ways of obtaining extra cash to increase your deposit. Open a bank account in which you will pay the funds for the deposit, and let it become your absolute priority. I call it an "investment account", rather than savings account. You gather the financial means that will change your future, so this is your investment. Savings are associated with something that you do long-term, in fact, your whole life. The name "investment account" changes your way of thinking and generate additional benefits.

Your deposit secures the bank against the loss in the case that you are unable to pay the mortgage, which may result in the property being repossessed by the bank. In this situation the bank would be forced to sell your property below its market value. Therefore, it requires a deposit of 5% or 10% of the house value (data for 2019). In the years 2003–2008, just before the housing bubble crash, banks were offering loans up to 125% of the property value. What did that mean? If you were buying a house for £100,000, you could get a loan of £125,000, therefore allowing you to renovate the property. Property prices were rising so fast, that banks believed there would be a profitable return on investment. This proved extremely risky, and in 2008 many properties were repossessed by banks. In another scenario, if you want to buy a property for £180,000, but your earnings allow for a mortgage of £150,000 – here you need a deposit of £30,000.

Paperwork needed for a mortgage

If you have a permanent job, you need documents like the ones needed when you rent out an apartment. Typically, the bank (or the broker that represents you) asks for the confirmation of the three-months income from your employer and payslips from your company. If you don't have a fixed salary, your bank may require payslips from the last six months, followed by bank statements from the last three months, and a copy of your passport or ID. You must also declare your monthly expenses so that the bank can assess your creditworthiness. Besides, you will need to confirm your home address (bank statements, utility bills from the last three months, for instance water, electricity, council tax etc.).

If you're self-employed or have more than 20% of shares in the company that employs you, until recently you needed a document from HMRC (SA302) for the last two years and your annual tax review, also for the last two years. Currently, a tax calculation is required. This can be generated from your HMRC online account, or you can ask your accountant to print this document out.

In addition, the lender will ask for an annual Tax Year Overview for the last two years. Directors of Limited companies may also be asked to provide the company's accounts or references from the company accountant.

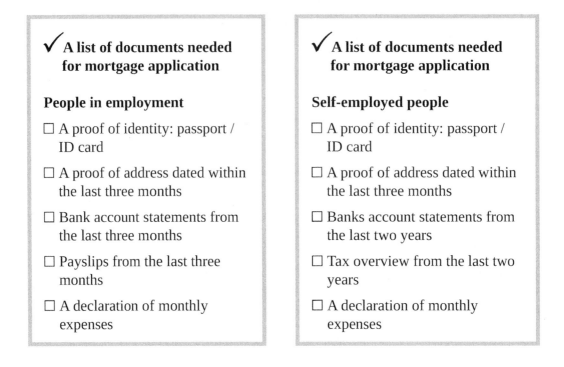

✓ **A list of documents needed for mortgage application**

People in employment

☐ A proof of identity: passport / ID card

☐ A proof of address dated within the last three months

☐ Bank account statements from the last three months

☐ Payslips from the last three months

☐ A declaration of monthly expenses

✓ **A list of documents needed for mortgage application**

Self-employed people

☐ A proof of identity: passport / ID card

☐ A proof of address dated within the last three months

☐ Banks account statements from the last two years

☐ Tax overview from the last two years

☐ A declaration of monthly expenses

Summary of the chapter:

1. Calculate what mortgage you can get.
2. Find out about different types of mortgages and choose the most suitable option.
3. Obtain the funds for your deposit. (The bigger the deposit, the bigger the chance for a better property with a lower interest rate.)
4. Check what paperwork you need when applying for a mortgage.

✏ *Exercise*

Saving money for a deposit must begin with wise purchasing decisions. Act sensibly and don't let yourself be carried away by emotions. Remember that every unnecessary item you buy will stand in the way of saving enough money. Before you go shopping, make a list of things that are absolutely necessary and stick to it. In addition, select 3 items that you can sell as soon as possible, and transfer the money from the sale to your deposit (investment) account.

. . . .

. . . .

. . . .

. . . .

. . . .

. . . .

. . . .

. . . .

. . . .

. . . .

. . . .

6. Repaying a mortgage

Before proceeding on taking out a mortgage, ensure that you are aware of all the changes that can occur whilst you're repaying the mortgage. Understand your position on repaying at either a slow or fast rate, price volatility, increase in interest rates and any restrictions. Once you have covered all areas then ensure you have a strategy for if things don't go to plan to avoid any pitfalls.

Repaying at a slow or fast rate; you can choose the option with flexible repayments. This allows you to reduce the repayment period, which is usually from 15 to 40 years. You can also make additional payments or reduce your monthly repayment for a limited time. Some lenders even allow you to freeze mortgage repayments, as is the case with cash loans available at every bank.

Impact on price volatility

The UK property market is one of the most mature in the world. It has undergone many crisis situations, but the government has always managed to find a way out. For example, reducing the Bank of England base rate to the lowest 0.25% in history (on the 11th of March 2020 The Bank of England base rate decreased from 0.75% to 0.25%, the government made mortgages affordable, or they manipulated stamp duty land tax regulations in favour of the buyers. On the 19th of March 2020, as a result of COVID-19 pandemic, the Bank of England lowered the rate again from 0.25% to 0.10%.

Prices in different towns and cities in the UK are lower compared to those in the capital, so for people who decided to buy the property there, the effects of the crisis were not as drastic. Nevertheless, it's best to be prepared for the possible fall in property prices, instead of panicking. During the crisis of 2008, half a million borrowers owned a property whose value dropped from a few to several dozen percent. Only the people who decided to sell quickly felt the impact of the crisis. Over the following years property prices have risen again, and the current value of these properties is in most cases several dozen percent higher than the purchase price.

✏ Exercise

An average three-bedroom house in North London in the Wood Green area, bought for between £260,000 and £300,000 in 2008, the year in which housing crisis took place, is currently valued at £500,000–£600,000, which means that over the past 10 years its value has increased almost twice (96% on average).

Another reason why it's safe to invest in the UK is because land prices are very high, especially in London. It's also difficult to get a building permit, and the demand for properties is continuously increasing.

Options for increase in interest rates

To begin with, you can choose a fixed rate mortgage, usually for a period of two to five years. Whether or not the Bank of England raises the base rate, your monthly repayment stays the same. If you intend to sell your property or plan to buy a larger one and let it out, check if there're early repayment charges on your mortgage. Such prepayment penalties can range from one to several percent of your mortgage.

The most popular way of dealing with an increase in interest rates is letting out a room or rooms. If you don't want to have tenants for a longer period of time, you can always let the room out for a few days, for example via such websites as www.airbnb.co.uk, www.holidaylettings.co.uk, and many others. There's also a possibility of letting out the whole house during the holiday season. Before you go, you could pack some of your belongings, put them in one room and let your house out for several weeks. This form of letting is very popular in large cities and in good locations close to the underground and the city centre.

Restrictions on residential mortgage

There're differences between buy-to-let and residential loans with respect to how they are regulated and secured, according to what criteria they are granted. Most importantly, they serve completely different objectives. A buy-to-let mortgage entitles you to let out the property you purchased. Attempting to let out a property with a residential mortgage is against its terms. In other words, if you have a residential mortgage, you cannot use it for letting out the property.

Mortgage/remortgaging advice: Mortgage Adviser

Mortgage & Protection Adviser Bartosz Laskowski is a Managing Director of Prestige Financial Advisers Ltd, a mortgage & insurance brokerage firm based in London and operating in the British Financial Services market since 2010. He is a landlord and property investor in Britain and Poland.

A monthly mortgage payment is one of the largest financial commitments in our monthly expenses. Hence, regular reviewing and checking the terms of the current mortgage loan agreement in comparison to offers available on the market is a must for those who care about their finances.

If you take into consideration an average UK mortgage of £123,423 (February 2018), a simple calculation will demonstrate that an interest rate reduction of just 0.5% will bring you savings of £600 annually on interest alone. Thus, with the same monthly repayment, you can pay off more of the actual debt, because a smaller proportion of the payment would cover interest and more will go towards the actual capital repayment. With the current property prices, the amount of debt is often much higher than £123,423, therefore the higher your mortgage, the more savings you can generate by changing the mortgage loan agreement to a new one with more favourable terms and interest.

The main solutions that can help are remortgaging and product switch. Could you please tell us about them?

Remortgaging is refinancing the debt: it's about transferring your current mortgage to another lender. It's a process that can usually get you the best savings, as banks and Building Societies often offer more preferential terms for new clients than for those who are already with them. The main advantage is, above all, the possibility to choose the best interest rate from the offers available on the market (there are currently over 80 lenders in the UK, so there's a lot to choose from). Remortgaging also gives you the opportunity to make other changes that may not be available with product switch, such as:

1. Changing the mortgage term

The interest rate is not always the main reason for changing the mortgage loan agreement. A mortgage is a long-term commitment, whereas our financial and personal circumstances may change over the years and it's often difficult to predict what will happen next. A promotion, additional funds that could possibly reduce your debt, or a thriving business? Remortgaging will make it possible to shorten the term of your mortgage, to which you will become debt-free faster. If, however, the forecast is not that optimistic, or you anticipate making an investment for which you will need more funds, you can extend the mortgage term and significantly lower the monthly repayment.

2. Borrowing more – renovation or purchase of a new property

Has your house become too small? Is some renovation needed? Or maybe you are considering buying another property? You can obtain additional equity for these projects by carrying out the remortgaging process. However, you should remember that your mortgage affordability and your property value must be sufficient.

3. Changing the type of mortgage

What about the situation when you want to make regular overpayments in order to pay off the debt faster and thus lower the monthly repayments, and your lender doesn't allow this? In this case remortgaging can be an answer. You should look for a mortgage that will meet your expectations. The same goes for situations when you only pay off interest on capital (interest-only mortgage), and you would like to start paying off capital as well (repayment mortgage).

4. Divorce or change of ownership

In the circumstances where a change of owner is required (for example due to divorce or parting with a partner) and one of the co-owners would like to buy out the property rights of the other, this is a good opportunity to review your mortgage loan agreement and change the lender to obtain the best deal.

5. Shared Ownership staircasing or Help to Buy (equity loan)

If you bought a property through the Shared Ownership scheme or a government's Help to Buy Equity loan and would like to become a 100% owner, you should definitely consider a comprehensive remortgaging process, so that the new mortgage is on favourable terms, and with the most suitable interest rate.

6. Debt consolidation

In some cases, remortgaging may be a good solution when you want to consolidate other debts. If you've recently had increased outgoings (for example due to renovation) and have had to use additional loans or credit cards, not necessarily on the most favourable terms, it may turn out that the interest you're paying for them is very high. One of the benefits of remortgaging is consolidating these high-interest loans or credit cards – this involves borrowing a specific amount to pay off these debts. This, of course, means your mortgage will be bigger and you must be careful.

What does remortgaging look like?

First of all, you need to define your main goal: is it maximum interest rate reduction, changing the term, additional borrowing, changing from interest only to repayment, or a combination of the above? It's also worth taking into account your longer-term plans for example, relocation, a sale of your property, or renovation, as these factors should also be considered when choosing a new mortgage.

There are several ways to change your mortgage loan agreement. You can compare the current offers on your own, through online comparison sites, or use the help of a mortgage broker. The second solution usually works best when you need expert advice, have limited time or insufficient market knowledge. When choosing a broker, make sure that they have appropriate experience and that they are a 'Whole of Market' mortgage broker, which means they have access to offers from the entire mortgage market.

Applying for remortgaging to a new lender is carried out in a similar way to purchasing a property. You must be prepared to present the bank with all the necessary documents and current situation in terms of earnings, financial liabilities, dependants or credit history. A valuation of the property will also be required to confirm its present condition and value. As soon as the bank or Building Society approves your application and is satisfied with the result of the valuation, they will issue a Mortgage Offer. To finalise a new mortgage loan agreement you will need a solicitor responsible for paying off the current loan and switching the mortgage from one lender to another, as well as reporting this change on the Land Registry. This is a much less complicated process than buying as usually there's no change of ownership. The whole process usually takes 4–6 weeks, so in order to avoid any rush, it's best to start acting at least 3 months before the end of the current deal.

What are the costs of remortgaging?

There's an early repayment fee associated with the change of a lender and repayment of the existing debt. Therefore, it's good to wait until the end of the fixed period agreed with the bank (usually 2 years) before you start the process of remortgaging. It's recommended to start your application 3 months before the end of the current agreement, and to complete it immediately after the expiry of penalty fees. Currently, most of the offers on the market exempt clients from fees for valuation and legal services, as it's covered by the new lender.

When choosing a new offer, you should also pay attention to the booking fee or arrangement fee, which can amount to several thousand pounds. You can find offers with very favourable interest rates but requiring an additional fee. It's worth calculating which option would be more beneficial – with or without extra fees. Also, when you hire a broker, most mortgage broking companies in the UK charge fixed, predetermined fees for their services. Few make their fee dependent on the value of the mortgage. You should pay attention to it, because it may not be favourable.

An alternative solution to remortgaging is product switch. Could you please tell us about it?

It's usually a less complicated process, which consists in changing the terms of the mortgage loan agreement while staying with the current lender. The main advantage of this option is the fast implementation time – the current lender usually doesn't require any documents or verification of your income. In addition, there's no actual mortgage change, so no solicitor is involved in the entire procedure.

Product switch can be done directly with your lender or with the help of a mortgage broker. This option is a good solution for those whose income has diminished and may have problems with obtaining sufficient financing from another bank. The main disadvantage of this option is the limited product choice – we can only use the products on offer from the current lender. Thus, the interest rate may not be as favourable as with another lender, and the terms of the new agreement may not be suitable for present situation or future plans.

It's also worth remembering that in case of the product switch, the current lender won't do a property valuation, as it will be usually based on average market prices (indexed value). This may automatically put you in a worse position if you've made significant changes and repairs at home increasing its value. A property valuation can improve your loan to value (LTV) ratio, and this automatically may result in a potentially better interest rate. By switching to a new deal with the same lender, we also have limited possibilities as to changes such as modification of the mortgage term or the type of repayment.

There's a lot of important information here. Let's summarise it now.

Summing up, full remortgaging and a change of the lender can give you more savings and access to more offers that will be more suitable for you. The procedure is slightly more time-consuming but taking into account that the monthly mortgage payment is usually our largest financial commitment, it's worth looking at the long-term benefits. Staying with the same lender and doing the product switch should be faster and without major formalities. However, we must be aware of the limitations as to changes to the terms of the mortgage loan agreement and the fact that the interest rate on the loan may not be as attractive as in the case of changing the lender.

You should also remember that once you've completed your first remortgaging, it's worth keeping your eyes wide open. Today's best deal may not be so in six months' time. That's why it's so important to keep your finger on the pulse or have a good mortgage broker to do it for you.

Thanks to the help of the Whole of market broker in the UK, Prestige Financial Advisers (prestigefs.co.uk), you can receive free initial and non-binding consultation to find out about your remortgage options. Each new client receives a free and non-binding initial consultation. They are a Whole of Market broker, which guarantees that your loan will be on the most favorable terms. This material is for information purposes and does not constitute a sales offer or financial advice. Before accepting any loan agreement, you must obtain individual advice regarding your own requirements and general terms of the loan.

Contribution by Bartosz Laskowski, contact details below:

Bartosz Laskowski

Mortgage & Protection Adviser
Prestige Financial Adviser
m: 075 8412 6487
w: pfadvisors.co.uk or prestigefs.co.uk
e: bartosz@pfadvisors.co.uk

Summary of the chapter:

1. Find out what you can do when the interest rate on your mortgage increases.
2. Make purchasing a property a step-by-step process (exercise on the next page).
3. Remortgaging and changing of lender can provide you with more savings.

✎ *Exercise*

Each goal needs to be broken down into steps. If the goal is too general, your brain receives information that it's not able to process. Divide the purchasing process into 4–8 steps. You can begin in the following way:

1. In the first week focus on understanding the concept of credit history; next, check yours and determine what you could do to make it look better.
2. In the following week analyse your earnings and arrange a broker who will check your creditworthiness. If it isn't satisfactory, plan what to do to increase your earnings, so that the bank lends you the amount you need.

Take a few minutes to write down your action plan.

. . . .

. . . .

. . . .

. . . .

. . . .

. . . .

. . . .

. . . .

. . . .

7. Credit history

In the UK there're three major **credit referencing agencies**: *Experian*, *Equifax* and TransUnion (formerly *Callcredit*). These're commercial agencies that collect personal data from many different sources and then sell it in the form of reports to financial institutions and consumers. This data includes, among others: name, date of birth, current and previous addresses, electoral register, history of your loan repayments, country court judgements, bankruptcies or administration orders, and house repossessions.

Based on reports from these agencies, banks as well as other institutions and businesses can issue decisions on granting credit cards, loans, mortgages, tenancy agreements, and even contracts for a new mobile phone. You can access a free report on your credit history at www.creditkarma.co.uk. The most important thing in this report is **your credit history**, which is a list of all your accounts (bank accounts, credit cards, business credits). Credit history also includes information such as the account's opening date, the credit limit you have, and confirmation that all payments have been made in a timely manner. This information stays in your report for six years, i.e. any late payment, even if it's the £5 minimum payment required on your credit card account, will be visible.

If you have an account with any of the above-mentioned agencies, you can find out about each institution that has checked your report. The report doesn't include information about your savings accounts, religion, medical history, criminal record, criminal past or a membership of a political party. Instead, you'll find out if your name is on the electoral register. If you haven't so far registered to vote, do it as soon as possible at www.gov.uk/register-to-vote.

Some lenders require this even before you apply for a mortgage. It's only based on the report that a credit institution can determine how financially responsible you are and assess how risky it'd be to lend you money. The reasons why your application might be rejected are: no credit history, too many loans, or frequent checking of your credit history within a short period of time by various institutions.

Each lender has its own criteria, so some lenders can reject your mortgage application and others can accept it. However, if many of your applications were rejected, this may be an issue. In this situation you shouldn't try to apply for more credit cards or open new bank accounts and take any loans for at least six months before buying your first property. It's important to think about this, because a bad credit history can make the bank think it'd be too risky to lend you the money. They may decline your application or offer interest rate up to several percent higher than the in case of a person with a good credit history.

You can check your **credit report** at any time, by registering on one of the agencies' websites as mentioned above. Usually a 30-day trial period option is available there, during which you'll have a free access to the report. However, if you want a permanent access, you'll need to pay a set fee per month or annum.

For the most accurate report that has information from all three credit referencing agencies, go to www.checkmyfile.com, and generate full pdf report. It is free for 30 days, then, if you wish to continue, the membership cost is £14.99 per month. In the credit reports you can also find financial "connections" with other people – spouse, family members, business partners. If it's unfavourable for you, and you're not legally responsible for the finances of these people, you can ask for this data to be deleted. This is usually done by sending an official letter requesting for the information to be removed.

Incorrect information in the credit report

You may not request the removal of truthful information from your credit report. However, you have the right to question any incorrect or inaccurate information concerning you personally. You'll then have to contact the company that is your creditor. For example, if you've decided to close your bank account and you have the confirmation that it's been closed, but it still appears in the report, you can send the confirmation to the credit referencing agency and ask them to remove outdated information.

Closing one of your credit card accounts and regular debt repayment will cause your credit scoring to increase. If it's fair, very good or excellent, you'll be classed as a potential low-risk borrower and the bank will offer you better credit terms. However, if the unfavourable information contained in the report is true, you'll still have the right to ask for a notice of correction (200 words) to be attached. If, for some reason, a credit referencing agency refuses to post this corrigendum, you can appeal to the Office of the Information Commissioner and check whether your entry has somehow violated the terms of the Data Protection Act.

If the report contains information confirming fraud, for example someone once had used your lost ID card, you should report it to all three credit agencies as soon as possible. If you had a problem with loan repayment in the past, you can approach charity associations like National Debtline or the Consumer Credit Counseling Service for help. These institutions can negotiate on your behalf debt cancellation or repayment in instalments, which may help you get a mortgage in the future.

Summary of the chapter:
1. Check your credit history by downloading a free
   report from www.creditkarma.co.uk. Or checkmyfile.com
2. If you find any information there that's inaccurate or untrue, please remove it. You can ask to attach your rectification to other information. In contentious cases you can appeal to the Office of the Information Commissioner.
3. If your name hasn't so far been included in the electoral register in the UK, register as soon as possible at www. gov.uk/register-to-vote. Some banks require a confirmation of your entry in the electoral register when applying for a mortgage.

✐ Exercise

In the previous exercise you've split your goal into steps. After completing each step, assess your activities by answering the questions:

1. Have you stuck to your plan?
2. Have you got enough time and resources to achieve this goal?
3. If you've answered "no" to the above questions – what can you do to secure these resources?
4. What have you learnt so far?
5. What possibilities open as you get closer to your goal?

. . . .

. . . .

. . . .

. . . .

. . . .

. . . .

. . . .

. . . .

. . . .

. . . .

. . . .

8. Government help scheme (Help to Buy)

There're several government programs in the UK that aim to help first-time buyers in the British Isles. The law and forms of help change from time to time, so it's best to keep track of this information on a regular basis. Currently (2020), the most popular programmes available are those described below.

1. Help to Buy Equity Loan – this is an interest-free government loan of up to 20% of the property value. It's interest-free for the first 5 years, so you won't incur any costs during this period. In other words, for the first five years you will have no costs related to the loan. After that the interest rate of 1.75% will be added to your repayments. With each subsequent year the interest rate will depend on the inflation rate – hence the cost may go up. If you have a cash deposit of (minimum) 5%, you can become a real estate owner with the help of Equity Loan. The program covers only new builds from registered developers.

The government pays up to 20% in the form of a cash loan, but the value of the property cannot exceed £600,000. Together with your own contribution, the additional funds make up a cash deposit of 25% necessary to apply for a mortgage. Remember that one of the criteria for using the program is having a satisfactory credit history. In London, due to very high property prices, the government increased the capital loan limit to 40% of the property value (London Help to Buy).

📖 Example

You found a house in London worth £300,000 that you'd like to buy. When you apply for a mortgage, you need a 5% deposit. If you prove that you have £15,000, the UK government will give you an interest-free loan of up to 40% of the value of your home for the period of 5 years.

With the house worth £300,000, this means £120,000. So, you need a mortgage of around £165,000. This means that your earnings must be around £40,000 a year (if you're buying as a married couple, your earnings together must amount to £40,000) to get a loan. The main condition, however, is that the property you plan to buy is newly built and its price may not exceed £600,000.

You don't need to be a first-time buyer to use Equity Loan. You can also apply if you're already a homeowner but you'd like to move to a new place. The regulations, however, prohibit you from subletting the property later, or from purchasing another property while using the program.

2. Shared Ownership – this is a scheme that allows you to buy a stake in a house, usually between 25% and 75%. It's a form of help for people who struggle with getting a mortgage for the full value of the property. There's an option of buying the rest of your shares in the future.

The scheme can be used to buy both newbuilds and older buildings (most programs only cover new buildings). There're two eligibility criteria. Firstly, you must have an annual income of at least £8,000, and secondly, you must be a first-time buyer. Therefore, **if you own a property in another country, then you don't qualify.** Shared Ownership properties are always leasehold, i.e. you become the owner of the property, but you don't own the land on which the property is located. Usually, the property is purchased jointly with a housing association; don't confuse it with a real estate agency. You can buy the rest of the property with your savings, or you can apply for a mortgage. You must pay the rent for the part of the property that you don't own, as it's now rented by you.

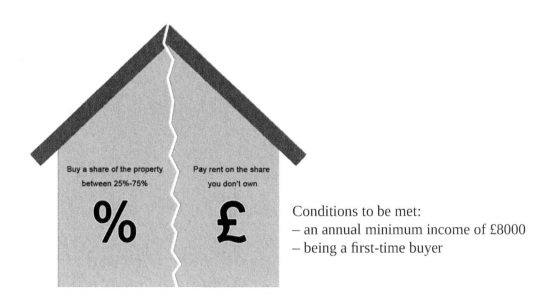

Buy a share of the property between 25%-75%

Pay rent on the share you don't own

%   £

Conditions to be met:
– an annual minimum income of £8000
– being a first-time buyer

3. Help to Buy ISA – the program closed for new applicants on the 30th of November 2019. If you've already opened a Help to Buy ISA account (or did so before 30 November 2019), you will be able to continue saving into your account until November 2029. How did it work? You started by paying in £1200 and then putting aside £200 a month. The moment you had £1600, you got a bonus of £400. From then on, for every £200 you saved, you'd get a £50-bonus.

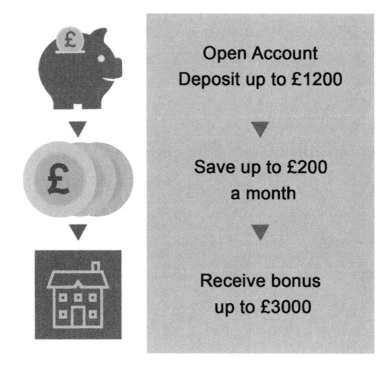

Open Account
Deposit up to £1200

▼

Save up to £200
a month

▼

Receive bonus
up to £3000

The maximum amount you could receive was £3000. If two people were buying, they could get up to £6000. Bonuses were never physically transferred into the buyer's account – they were transferred to the account of the solicitor who represented the first-time buyer.

4. Right to Buy – if you rent your property from your local council, you can apply for buying it with a huge discount. Usually, the minimum period you need to rent the property from the council is 3–5 years. The discount can amount to £82,800 in England and up to £110,500 in London. Most of the banks will accept this discount as your deposit, so you usually don't need your own financial contribution to apply for a mortgage. When the discount is being determined, the council considers factors such as the rental period from the council and the current value of the property. After the purchase it's usually not possible to sell the property for the first 5 years, as you'd have to pay back all, or part of, the discount received.

You're usually allowed to borrow four to five times your annual income, so if you earn £25,000 a year, you should look for a property for around £112,500. More information and updates regarding these programs can be found at www.helptobuy.gov.uk.

Summary of the chapter:
1. Find out which programs are currently being offered by the British government to help first-time buyers in Great Britain. Check which one you could be entitled to.

✎ *Exercise*

In the past, financial security was guaranteed by material goods. Now, it's worth investing in skills. Write down two competences you need to gain to start earning more. Then write how you intend to gain them (reading books, blogs, completing courses, training, talking to specialists in a given field). Set a time frame and start implementing your plan.

. . . .

. . . .

. . . .

. . . .

. . . .

. . . .

. . . .

. . . .

. . . .

. . . .

. . . .

. . . .

9. How to find your dream home

When viewing a house, you must make sure it's habitable. Even if the house needs to be renovated, its technical condition should make it possible to use the rooms for their intended purpose. This means that despite a lower standard, the bathroom and kitchen must be workable – even if they're antique. **If the technical condition of rooms doesn't allow for their proper functioning, it'll be more difficult for you to get a mortgage.**

A helpful tool during the process of choosing the perfect home is creating **a list of criteria** to consider while making your decision. It's best to split the list into two columns:

"I'D LIKE IT TO BE" and "MUST HAVE".

My ideal home

I'd like it to be	Must have
. . . .	. . . .
. . . .	. . . .
. . . .	. . . .
. . . .	. . . .

You will find several examples of the criteria you can apply below. Read them and decide which column they belong under:

- The location of the house, facing south or west – depending on that, the garden gets the sun in the morning or in the afternoon
- Neighbourhood – who lives nearby
- Schools in the area – what's their Ofsted ranking
- Local shops and supermarkets
- Quiet / loud neighbours
- Parking place /garage
- Access to public transport
- Room sizes
- Housing or commercial estate
- Crime rate
- Number of bathrooms and whether there's a separate toilet
- Parks in the area

Location – this is one of the most important criteria when choosing a house, and its choice depends on several different factors. Consider whether you want to live in the middle of a specific district or in a specific part of the city, or if you prefer the outskirts. Think about the distance between the property, your work and your children's school. Also, would the facilities such as a bus stop, train station, shops, or a gym be within the right range for you? If you work from home, will your clients have easy access and enough parking spaces?

🔔 Remember!

If this is an investment in your future, location is key. In the UK it's better to buy a lower-standard house but in a good location. A house on a main street may cost less AND have better access to transport.

When you decide to sell your property, you may find that people are less willing to buy it; however, renting it out can prove to be very profitable. Tenants usually look for a dwelling close to the underground station, bus stop and shopping facilities, so the house located on the main street is very convenient.

I don't recommend buying close to the railway or underground tracks. Firstly, it can be loud, and secondly, there're often more cracks on the walls. Sometimes Japanese knotweed, a plant that can cause problems to the structure of the building, grows along the tracks. It's difficult to get rid of it, and if the plant grows seven meters from the border of your plot, getting the mortgage is virtually impossible.

Number of rooms – when choosing a house, you must decide how many rooms you need. Maybe you need just one, but you'd like to rent out two extra rooms. This can be a good way of financing your mortgage repayment. Consider, whether you'd need an additional bathroom for tenants. The smallest room in the house (box room) can be offered to someone without paying rent. In return, your tenant can help with your household chores, and you'll have more time to focus on earning money to buy another house.

Garden – think how important it's for you to have a garden. If it's an essential element of your new home, you must pay attention to its condition and size. If you don't need it, you can buy a cheaper property, and thus pay off a lower mortgage and have an extra budget, for example for travelling.

Garage – even if you don't have a car, a house with a garage can be a good option. In most houses the garage can be converted into an additional room, bathroom or even a small studio apartment. After a few small changes, you could have an additional income from renting out an additional room.

Parking space – if you don't have a car, you don't need a parking space, but it can be useful. If you choose a house near an underground station, you may be able to rent it to people who work in the city centre and want to park their car during the day.

Helpful tips

Pros and cons of location:

1. **Check what happens in the neighbourhood in the morning and evening.** Some post codes or streets have a reputation for being unsafe. It's also possible that the same street up to a certain number is ok and has a reputation of a good neighbourhood, whereas its other end is a gathering place for people not necessarily carrying out respectable activities and maybe considered unsafe.

2. **Check on the website of your local council whether the area where you want to buy is classed as a regeneration area.** It's not uncommon that in such areas new attractive buildings are being built, council authorities renovate the sidewalks and /or the local shopping centre, create gyms in the parks, or open a new railway station. Thanks to these investments, the value of your property will increase over the next few years.

3. **Look for a partner.** If the house in your chosen location is out of your reach, you can always buy with a friend, a partner or even with another family member. However, before deciding to buy with others, you should first set the rules and sign an agreement.

4. **Agree to compromise.** There's little chance of finding a property that meets all your requirements. In the British TV show *Location, Location, Location* Phil Spencer advises to master the art of compromise. His advice is to focus on the three most important elements (home triangle), namely budget, size and location. An ideal home should meet at least one of these criteria.

I believe that the house that doesn't meet all the criteria should motivate us to set a new goal. Personally, I'd keep looking for a dream home, and gradually adapt the one I live in for letting out.

🔔 **Remember!**

Success is a journey, not a destination. Looking for the perfect house can take several years and become an unforgettable adventure. It's better to invest your money on a regular basis, instead of saving for years to buy your dream home.

House prices are rising on a year-to-year basis, and when you set aside money without actively multiplying it, instead of getting closer to the purchase, your goal will start moving away from you. For this reason, it's worth considering a fast purchase of a small property, the value of which will increase in time. After some time, you'll be able to sell it and use the previously invested deposit plus what you've earned on the sale to buy a new property. Alternatively, you can change your residential mortgage into BTL and start generating rental income.

Checking for pest presence

Before you decide to buy a given property, **check it for bed bugs, cockroaches, wasps, fleas, rats** and other intruders. While the wasp nest is quite easy to spot, bedbugs and cockroaches are usually less visible. Look carefully at every nook and cranny and pay attention to furniture, because insects can also be found inside wardrobes, cupboards etc. If you have any doubts, ask the owner for a current report from a pest control company. After completing the purchase arrange a visit of pest control company and request disinfestation, disinfection or rodent control.

Things look different when it comes to **bats.** They're legally protected, and if you remove them yourself, you can be fined at least £5000. If you want to get rid of bats in the attic, you must contact a company that offers such services. Before that you should seal up all the openings, holes in the roof, walls and other entry points. The company will construct a special booth, which will be placed in the garden. If the bats don't find a way back into the attic, they'll relocate into that booth, which after some time will be moved to another place.

In case of larger investments, you should apply to Natural England Licensing for a special license. It'll specify the manner and system of works related to the construction, least interfering with the bats.

Another potential issue are grass snakes. This species is also protected, and you can be fined up to £5000 for its removal. As with bats, you need to contact a specialist company to take care of it. If the grass snakes can be found within a larger area, a special group of environmentalists will collect them for 20 consecutive days. After a 7-day break, if no grass snake is spotted, the area is seen as "clean".

A major threat, interfering with the building's structure, is dry rot. It's a kind of fungus attacking moist boards and beams found in the walls and floors. Sometimes it can't be spotted with the naked eye. A worrying sign may be, for example, rectangular cracks on painted parts of the wood, such as skirting boards at home. You should also pay attention to the red-coloured coating of boards. Another way of checking if a house is infected with dry rot is using dry rot sensors. These are small metal rods that resemble nails, which are stuck in the wood with patches of mould. The sensors are saturated with chemicals which change colour while reacting with dry rot.

If you find dry rot, you need to replace the infected part of the wooden structures with a new one. This work will be expensive, merely painting the infected wood won't solve the problem.

Checking the neighbourhood

You can save a lot of time and money if you're well prepared to buy a house. Firstly, before the viewing, carefully check the neighbourhood. Learn the opinions about a given street. Go and check what's going on there in the morning and in the evening. Try to figure out the condition of nearby houses. Check the area from every possible angle, considering even small details that could affect the price of the house. Try to answer the following questions:

- Are house fronts neat?
- Are there good schools in the area?
- What's the traffic like?
- What's the price of renting a similar-sized house?
- Do the flats for sale belong to the group of ex-council dwellings?

You can find information such as **house prices on a given street**, as well as the prices of houses sold since 1995. You can also track the prices of a specific property on the Rightmove website using the Property Log tab in the Google Chrome plug-in.

My favourite way of checking the house in terms of risks is to try to obtain a free building insurance quote. You can quickly get a quote after entering data such as the address and size of the house (or several other parameters). If the insurance quote is very high, it may mean that your street has problems with the structure of buildings or foundations, or floods have been reported in the past, or the area has a high crime rate.

You can verify the crime rate at www.police.uk. When reviewing the data, pay attention to whether there's a lot of supermarkets in the area. This fact can have a direct impact on the statistics, because it can be petty crimes, for example children stealing small things from the supermarket, and this shouldn't really discourage you from buying a house.

To verify the property, I'd also recommend www.checkmystreet.co.uk. After entering the post code of the neighbourhood you're interested in, you'll have access to information about a given council. For example, you can check where the nearest underground stations, train stations or bus stops are, and how much time you'd need to get there. Often, the results also show the average price for renting a property in this area, and the sale price of houses in the previous years.

On this page you'll also find local crime rate subdivided into categories such as: incidents, anti-social behaviour, vehicle crime burglaries and other serious criminal offences. There's also information on broadband availability in the area, its maximum speed, as well as the possibility of connecting to superfast broadband (fibre broadband).

I also recommend using www.propertydata.co.uk. After entering the post code you'll find all the statistical data and you can calculate the average rate of return on your investment. You'll find out about the average rent for a one-bedroom flat (1 bed) and two-bedroom flat (2 bed). You'll also get data such as: the average purchase price, the most profitable type of properties, the average price of properties, number of cars per family, demographic information, the preferred type of transport in the neighbourhood, and whether owners or tenants live around.

10. Where to look for a property?

Here are the websites where you can find interesting offers:
— www.zoopla.co.uk
— www.rightmove.co.uk
— www.onthemarket.co.uk
— www.primelocation.com

Zoopla and Rightmove websites also show houses that will be put on auction. Auction announcements are usually misleading, because instead of the actual selling price there's usually only guide price there. At the property auction, houses are usually sold for a price of several tens of thousands of pounds higher than the guide price. There's also a lot of risk involved, so I don't recommend buying at auction for inexperienced buyers. However, if you decide to purchase a property in this way, remember that you'll have to pay a 10% deposit on the day of the auction, and then you have 28 days to finalise the transaction.

Undoubtedly, you'll see **advertisements of properties for sale marked as repossessed**. These are the properties taken over by the bank (lender) because the original owner wasn't repaying the mortgage according to agreed rules. They're usually sold below their market value, because the lender wants to recover lost money as soon as possible. You could recognize them in the pictures by the white tape covering everything and the inscription: "No device has been tested by the estate agent."

Usually also gas and electricity are cut off. This type of properties usually requires major renovation works, so it's very important to factor the potential modernisation cost in the total purchase cost. Buying such a property you can, however, apply for a mortgage. The bank is usually understanding and doesn't impose any deadlines (unlike for a house bought at auction). Not infrequently, a deadline is also set for submitting bids.

Estate agencies

Contrary to popular belief, estate agencies can prove very helpful. In the Internet era it might seem that all properties for sale appear on specialist websites as soon they are put up for sale, but that's not the case.

Just imagine:
You work in an estate agency. A nice couple comes by. They talk to you about their dream home; moreover, they have two kids in school X, and they'd really appreciate a particular location. You know their names, you know what they look like and what they do. A seller comes by – he has a house in the area and signs a sales contract with you. What would you do? Would you put the sales advert online? Or would you call this nice family to help them make their dream come true?

Each estate agency has a list of registered clients and those clients, especially if they come in person, will be put on a priority list.

🔔 **Remember!**
To find a suitable house, you can hire a property sourcer or a property search agent. Their job is to search for ideal properties for others.
If you hire such a person, you can save a lot of time and money. However, if time isn't an issue and you've done your homework, it's best to do it on your own.

Viewing

It's good to be prepared to view the property, especially if you want to see more than two houses on the same day. Look at the floor plan to see if changes were possible. For example, you could divide the largest room into two smaller ones if needed (for example, if you have two children).

If you view a lot of properties on the same day, you can easily get the facts wrong. It's best to make notes, writing down the most important aspects. Some things are irrelevant, for example furniture, curtains or pictures on the walls. The property is usually empty when you collect the keys, so if you'd like something to be left there, you can include this in your purchase offer. It's important, however, in which direction the house is facing, because this determines whether you'll have sun in the garden or kitchen in the morning or in the afternoon. Most days on the British Isles are grey and without sun, so it'd be great to increase the chances of extra light.

If you want to have more sunlight in the morning, look for a house with windows facing the east. If you want to have more sunlight in the afternoon, when you come back from work – look for a house with windows facing the south or the west. It's best when the living room has a window at the front and at the back of the house, because then you'll have more sunlight throughout the day. Ideally, the property should be inhabited by its owners, as it'll be better looked after.

⌂ Remember!

If you're interested in buying a house, you can arrange a second viewing to check all the items on your list and ask for other details concerning owners or tenants.

When you assess a property, pay attention to the following:

Is there a central heating, new boiler, connection to the gas grid? If there's no gas supply in the house, the cost of connecting to the gas grid amounts to around £5000.

– What's the condition of the windows?
– Are there any leaks?
– What's the condition of kitchen and bathroom?
– Is there a church on the same street? If that's the case, I recommend buying chancel insurance, so that you don't have to pay contributions for the renovation of the church and church square.
– Do all fixtures and fittings work? If not, it'll be a good reason for offering a lower price.
– What's the condition of the building's structure inside and outside?

This will be checked thoroughly by a bank appraiser, but if you notice large cracks and splitting of the building, it's better to resign from the purchase.

– What's the condition of the roof?
– What does the garden look like? Ask which part of the fence will be your responsibility if you become the owner, because this is often arbitrary. Sometimes the information can be found in the land registry.
– Is there enough space to put a bed in the box room?
– If there's no room in the attic, is the highest roof point at 2.2 m? It's important in case you'd plan for an extension through the roof in the future.
– Is there damp or dry rot inside?

This could be a serious problem but not impossible to be solved (more on that at the end of the book).

– Are there any problems at home with ventilation and humidity levels caused by not opening windows or frequent drying of the laundry?
– Is the water pressure right in taps and the shower?
– Are there any rodents, bed bugs, fleas or cockroaches?

− Is it possible to install a satellite dish? In some blocks of flats there's only access to the main antenna, without the possibility of installing your own device.

You should arrange a second viewing at a different time of the day and pay attention to other features of the house. If during the viewing there's music turned on, the seller may want to hide the fact that the neighbours are loud or have a barking dog, or that there's a train passing by every few minutes or you can hear the landing / taking off planes. Burning candles and the scent of coffee may indicate problems with drainage or mice infestation. Check for cracks in the walls or dampness, usually behind a wardrobe. Take a note of how much available space there is for all the things you need only seasonally (storage), such as Christmas decorations or sports equipment. It's good to ask someone from your family or a friend to accompany you. Another person's opinion – unbiased and not driven by emotions – is priceless.

Think about questions for the current owner or tenant. Ask them what they would change or do in a given house, if they had £25,000. A person who currently lives in a house has lots of ideas and knows how to make it more comfortable, what could be done to get extra light or space. You should also ask about the lease and what would be the cost of extending it for another 10, 20, 25 years, who manages the building (whom you would be paying ground rent, building insurance etc.). You can ask about the rough cost of gas, electricity, and water, as well as council tax.

Also try to find out if the property has a parking space assigned, what renovation works have been carried out in recent years, whether there's a works guarantee, and whether any construction works are planned (this is especially important in case of blocks of flats, because the costs could amount to several thousand pounds; a solicitor should inform you about this). Ask if the current owner has made an insurance claim, if the building has had problems with cracks or subsidence and get to know the strengths and weaknesses of the area. The more you know, the more confident you'll be about the purchase.

It's also worth checking what the rental price of the property would be, if you ever decided to move. You can get to know the neighbourhood by simply walking there for 10–15 minutes. You'll see whether your neighbours have neat front gardens, how much time you need to get to the nearest store, school, post office, train station or underground, whether there're nice parks and playgrounds in the area in case you have children. If you don't have children yourself, remember that your future tenants could be a family with children, so it's worth knowing if such amenities are available.

Phil Spencer's book *How to Buy Your First Home* says that the most common reasons for selling a property are the so-called three Ds: debt, divorce and death. Such vendor is strongly motivated to sell faster, which gives you more possibilities as far as the price is concerned. As the saying goes: *Opportunities come to those who are prepared.* If you know the area and the value of the property, if you have a vision of how it can be expanded in the future and how much the house could be worth then, knowing how much you could sell or rent it for can earn good money.

People often ask me: *Is it ethical to offer a lower price to someone who's in a difficult position because of debt?*

◆ **My answer is always as follows:**

Put yourself in the position of the other person. If the house wasn't sold, the bank would repossess it. If it's sold to you, the owner will be able to repay the loan and thus settle the issue. Moreover, if he manages to sell the house for more than the mortgage and the fees for the solicitor and the agency, he'll still get some of the money. The key to a good business transaction is learning how to solve other people's problems.

Determining the actual price

The price of a property doesn't always reflect its value. Estate agencies can advise for how much a given property should be put up for sale, but the final decision is always made by the owner. So, while looking for a house with a budget amounting to £200,000, you should also view those for £230,000. There are neighbourhoods where houses priced at £200,000 are sold for much more, because block viewings or open days helped to increase the price.

If the property is in an area where the demand is very high, agencies would most often arrange viewings for the same day to drive up the price. This, however, shouldn't discourage you, because it often happens that nobody makes an offer – people think that because of so much interest their offer won't have clout. What's more, those who come to the viewing may want to eliminate competition by creating the appearance of high interest and in this way discourage other interested parties.

Check the prices of homes sold in the area via any of the following websites (www.rightmove.co.uk, www.zoopla.co.uk or www.mouseprice.com), but **also ask the estate agent**, whether in their opinion the price reflects the value of the property, and why. A given house can be more expensive than others on the same street since it's been renovated, it has a new kitchen and an additional bathroom, it has a converted attic or garage, or it's generally more spacious than other houses on the street.

In case of a flat, the price depends mainly on the number of years remaining in the lease. Despite this fact, having knowledge of sold prices in the area with a given post code **you can negotiate a lower price.** Not infrequently, estate agencies put up houses for sale with guide price only – this is the price range within which the seller wants to receive offers from prospective buyers.

If you think a given property is worth more – or is worth less – than the proposed price, but facts – and not emotions – indicate this would be a good investment, make an offer. The estate agent's duty is to get the best possible price for their client (vendor), so when negotiating with you, they just do their job well. In most cases, if you offer, say £150,000 and the agent immediately replies that they have much higher offers, this is usually the truth. On the other hand, if you hear that the vendor hasn't accepted the offer but would accept it if it were £160,000, then there's space for you to negotiate the price.

Don't do 100 viewings before you decide to buy. I can say this based on my own experience – I viewed 107 properties before I bought the one I'm currently living in. I also made several offers before, but they were rejected. Trust me – rejection of your offer shouldn't discourage you from action. Going for viewings, you learn and gain experience. Go to viewings with your notebook and write down all the information. Analyse your notes, see what you paid attention to and what you didn't notice previously.

🔔 **Remember!**

In England and Wales submitting an offer doesn't oblige you to buy a property (apart from buying at the auction). However, if you buy a property in Scotland, the offer is binding, and the seller may ask for compensation if you pull out. You can find more information at www.adviceguide.org.uk.

Summary of the chapter:

1. Compile a list of criteria according to which you'll assess and select the properties.
2. Check whether the selected property is pest-free. If this is not the case, find out what the problem is and what you can do.
3. Check the neighbourhood in which your property is located.
4. Consider hiring a property sourcer or property search agent to find a suitable house for you.
5. Prepare for a viewing.
6. Arrange a second viewing at a different time of the day and come with someone unbiased.
7. Negotiate the price.
8. Submit offers and learn from experience.

✎ *Exercise*

Look at the goal you've written down previously. Note all the benefits associated with it – in terms of time, material gains, emotional investment, relations and status. Becoming aware of these benefits will help you spot more opportunities, and this, in turn, will motivate you to act.

. . . .

. . . .

. . . .

. . . .

. . . .

. . . .

. . . .

. . . .

. . . .

. . . .

. . . .

. . . .

11. How to make an offer

It's best to make an offer in a written form, by email. The more information you provide about yourself, the more professionally you will be dealt with. **Ideally, the email should include the following**:
– your name, surname, address, contact details
– address of the property you're interested in
– enclosed confirmation of your deposit money
– details of your solicitor and mortgage broker (telephone numbers and e-mail addresses)
– mortgage in principle (if you already have it). This is a statement from the bank saying how much money you can borrow with your current earnings (you can ask your bank, any other bank or a mortgage broker for such a document – personally, I recommend asking the broker).

If your offer is accepted, **the agency will send you memorandum of sale (information memorandum)**, which includes details of seller and buyer, details of the agency and of both solicitors, confirmed purchase price, and date. Give this memorandum to your solicitor and mortgage broker.

Solicitor checks & requirements

To begin with, solicitors will ask for a passport or an ID card, a proof of address (for example, a utility bill), and an advance, usually around £300. Next, they will send a client care letter and a purchase questionnaire. The **purchase questionnaire** will contain standard information about you, such as your personal details, contact details, National Insurance Number. It will also include questions and issues such as follows:

- Fixtures and fittings – do you have a list of things, furniture, and appliances that were agreed with the seller as part of the house purchase?
- Do you need a mortgage, and if so, in which bank have you submitted your mortgage application, and for what amount?
- Before the completion, you must purchase a building insurance. The solicitor will ask if you have a broker who would deal with it. If not, you must confirm that you'll do it yourself.
- What kind of ownership will you choose if you don't buy on your own (joint tenants, tenants in common)?
- Would you like your solicitor to make any enquires on your behalf?
- Have you noticed any changes in the house, for example extension, replaced doors or windows?
- In order to pay your Stamp Duty Tax, the solicitor will ask you whether you have other properties or is that your first purchase. Do you need to sell any other property to buy a new one?
- Are you or your family a Politically Exposed Person (PEP)? Is anybody from your closest surroundings a Member of Parliament, a politician, or a person holding a high military rank?
- Where does the money for the deposit come from? Usually there're some options listed, and most people would indicate: 'My/our own savings'; remember, however, that you must be able to prove it. It's not uncommon for a solicitor to ask for the account statements showing deposit money from the past six months.
- What's the name of your bank, and what are the details of people who're registered with this account?
- What are the details of your employer?
- Would you like to have a will prepared after you buy a property?

You'll be also asked if you're buying the property on your own or with another person. If you're buying a house with another person, you must choose a property title, which will affect your tax return.

The solicitor will ask you to choose one of the following forms of ownership:
- **Joint tenants**, where the property is owned jointly by two or more parties (each party has equal rights to the whole property). In the event of one person's death, the full title is automatically transferred to the other person.
- **Tenants in common**, where each party owns separate shares of the property. Co-owners determine their shares in the house, and after their death the shares will be subject to inheritance regulations along with the rest of their assets.

The solicitor will check the title deed – whether the seller is the actual owner, and whether the property is not encumbered by any claims, liabilities or legal obligations such as court judgements or loans. Next, they will order checking the legal status of the property in the Land Registry and apply additional searches, not just legal ones. Among others, this will involve sending inquiries to the local council to check whether any construction work has been carried out on the property. If work was carried out they will check whether the owner had a permission to do so, and commissioning an environmental search to confirm whether there're any environmental risks or imbalances. Next, the solicitor will check the water supply system and verify whether the property is on ecclesiastical land.

The above searches are meant to ensure that the purchase of the property is a good decision from the legal point of view. If the property is unencumbered, the seller's solicitor will issue a document confirming that on the day of completion the obligations will be removed from it. This means that the money from the purchase will first cover the repayment of debts to banks or other institutions having charge on the property, and the surplus will be transferred to the seller's account. The participation of solicitors in such transactions, especially if you apply for a mortgage, is necessary, because they represent both the buyer and the lender that grants the mortgage. The lender doesn't cover any costs related to legal services – these need to be paid by the buyer.

Costs & contracts

The cost of legal service is between £700 and £1200 plus VAT. The solicitor fee depends on the type of property you buy and the location of the office (those with London addresses are the most expensive). Surveys usually cost around £250–£400. Then you must cover the costs of registration in the Land Registry, usually £40–£200, depending on the price of the property (there're also transactions with a fee close to several thousand pounds, for houses which were purchased for several million pounds). Other costs include submitting a tax return (around £80), bank transfers and postal services (around £30). The highest cost is the stamp duty tax, from which you can be exempt when you are a first-time buyer and you qualify for the stamp duty exemption applicable in 2020.

You pay the legal fees after the completion of the transaction. The deposit is paid just before the exchange of contracts, which usually takes place around 6–8 weeks from the beginning of the purchase process. Sometimes this process takes several months, for example, when someone inherits a house (probate) or a bank sells a repossessed house. It's possible that the seller's solicitor delays the delivery of the required documentation or there's a chain transaction involved, i.e. the seller is buying from someone who's waiting for the purchase of another property, etc.

It may also be that the solicitor faces **problems** discussed below.

– Surveys show some irregularity, for example a house has a garage that's been converted into a studio apartment without a planning permission, and you must decide whether to apply for a permit or convert it back into a garage.

– Despite the fact that you've received a mortgage in principle, the bank requires a lot more documents from you, for example current account statements to confirm your current expenses and costs.

– The seller decides not to sell the house or to sell it to someone else. In this case, the would-be buyer bears the costs of legal services provided so far, as well as the valuation fee, if they chose the option to pay for it (instead of it being covered by the bank).

Before signing the contract, it's a good idea to arrange another viewing of the property. Usually, the seller commits to carry out an inventory of equipment which will be left in the property, such as: built-in wardrobes, refrigerators, the oven, or sometimes, all the furniture. You can also ask for all the contents to be taken away. If that's the case, make sure that the house hasn't been vandalised when removing built-in elements

---

🔔 **Remember!**

You buy a property in the condition that you see on the day the contracts are exchanged, and not when you first view the house. So, you can arrange another viewing just before the exchange day.

You usually sign the contract much earlier, but it has no legal force until **the contracts are exchanged** between the seller's and buyer's solicitors. You won't be present at this exchange. This is usually done virtually and is confirmed by a telephone call, during which the solicitors set the date and time of contracts' exchange, confirm that all the information is correct and agreed on by both parties, and arrange the completion date. This date is agreed in advance with the seller and buyer and is confirmed by e-mail on the same day. **From this point on, you cannot change your decision without legal consequences.** If the buyer gives up the purchase, they lose the deposit, usually the 10% of the price of the property. If the seller pulls out, they must pay a penalty, the amount of which depends on what's specified in the contract during the exchange of contracts. Most often, it's 10% of the property price.

Solicitor Q&A Session: conveyancing process

1. Please can you take the reader through step by step the process of what's involved with first time purchase from your perspective?

Step 1 – Initial instructions from yourself (start)
To begin the conveyancing process of buying a house a solicitor needs to be instructed. They will then ask the buyer and seller to complete initial paperwork, provide their identify, address and source of funds documentation and finally provide initial monies on account to enable searches to be submitted.

Step 2 – Receive draft contract
The draft contract pack will be completed by the seller's solicitors and then sent to buyer solicitor. The contract will include; official copies (electronic deeds), property forms and duplicates of all relevant documents for that property.

Step 3 – Searches and investigation of title
The third step of the conveyancing process is the carrying out of searches that have been requested and the paperwork received from the seller's solicitor is reviewed. In the event that any queries about the property or paperwork are required then they are submitted to the seller's solicitor and the solicitor may need to refer to the seller. This process can be quite lengthy depending on a number of enquiries needed.

Step 4 – Report
Once all replies and the results of the searches are received, a report can then be created on the property and sent to the buyer along with the mortgage offer. The financial requirements of the transaction will also be detailed in a completion statement highlighting the total amount due to complete.

Step 5 – Signing

When you are happy with all the paperwork, we can then arrange for you to sign and a completion date is then decided amongst all parties involved in the transaction. At this stage in the conveyancing process, you will transfer the deposit, usually 10% of the purchase price, which enables exchange the contracts.

Step 6 – Exchange of contracts

The transaction and completion date become legally binding on the exchange of contracts. The deposit will be sent to the seller's solicitor and a request for your mortgage advance will be paid from the lender. Before completion, the balance of the funds due must be with the buyer solicitor at least one working day beforehand.

Step 7 – Conveyancing process for buying a house (finish)

Completion happens on the moving day and when the full purchase price is transferred to the Seller's solicitor. The keys are left with the estate agent and once the seller's solicitor has received the funds the keys are released.

2. How much does solicitors work cost? Please explain for both freehold and leasehold.

This is a very subjective question. Our website does set out the standard fees associated with a freehold/leasehold transaction which may be of more use. I would make a few key observations here:

– The fees are generally particular to the transaction details i.e. sale and purchase, redemption, mortgage, new build, complicated estate management areas, unregistered land as such. Whilst there might be an average fee, each transaction is different from the other so the fees will vary.
– Fees do vary based on the property value as with the change in value there is also a change in the risk associated with the legal responsibilities of the property as such a higher value property will cost more from a legal perspective.
– There are a plethora of online conveyancing teams offering minimal fees/ no completion no fee quotes – simply put, you pay for what you get and we have

heard 9/10 of clients who have used these services would never do so again as such whilst a firm such as ours has higher fees we offer a one to one service and relationship you won't get from online conveyancing.

3. How long does the process usually take, what can cause a delay?

Nowadays average is 6–10 weeks. Delays can occur due to multiple dependencies – from delays of the client completing their documentation, searches from the local council can take 2–4 weeks, a mortgage survey and approval can take several weeks, a large number of enquiries being required and responses being slow from a vendor, agreeing a completion (move in) date with a chain.

4. Please can you explain what a 'chain' is and how to be efficient if the reader is part of it?

A chain is a linked list of property transactions which depend on each other. At one end of the chain is a buyer who has no property to sell and at the other end of the chain is a seller who is not buying another property. When there are only two properties, then there is no chain. When there are three or more properties then there is a chain. Those in between the first buyer and the last seller are the links in the chain.

Where a delay occurs in the chain it will also delay everyone behind and ahead in the chain. Because it is a requirement for all contracts in a chain to exchange on the same day and for all money in a chain to be transferred at the same time, then if any person in the chain holds up the process, then no-one in the chain can exchange or complete. Everyone in the chain has to be ready to exchange and complete before the process can proceed.

By way of example; if a person is delayed by their mortgage then the remainder of the chain is also held up in the same delay. As such it is important to note it may not be in the power of the agent, solicitor or buyer/seller in one transaction that causes delay but someone further up or down the chain.

To be efficient; a buyer / seller should do everything as quickly as possible i.e. complete their paperwork, arrange their mortgage, conduct surveys inspections early on and answer any questions raised of them. Key is also to be flexible to complete as with a larger chain comes more peoples plans and desires as to dates to complete. if one person is difficult then it impacts everyone.

5. Please can you touch base on the lender panel list, what is it, how does it work?

All mortgage companies maintain a panel of solicitors who they are prepared to instruct. When a firm is not on a particular lender's panel they cannot act for that lender. It is generally quicker and cheaper if the same solicitor acts for both the buyer and the buyer's lender. If a separate solicitor is acting for the lender the buyer's solicitor paperwork will have to be sent back and forth between them, causing delays in the conveyancing. The buyer will also have to pay two lots of solicitor's fees. Generally a firm is required to have a minimum number of partners and the right insurance to act for a lender to be admitted to their panel. As we meet these requirements we generally find we are on most panels and can be admitted to any that we are not i.e. a new lender that enters the market.

Contribution by Bradley Moran – Solicitor

Summary of the chapter:
1. The purchase offer should be in writing, by e-mail.
2. You'll need a solicitor to represent you in your dealings with the lender and the seller.
3. Before you sign the purchase contract, you should view the property once again.
4. After the exchange of contracts between the solicitors, neither party can change the decision without legal consequences.

✏ *Exercise*

Positive habits are automated responses to stimuli. Forming a new habit will take from 3 to 4 weeks. Pick a habit today that will help you achieve your goal. If you'd like to have more time to explore the subject of real estate investment, you can start waking up an hour earlier than usual. Write below what habit you're going to develop from today on. Make a list of 2–3 things, which will motivate you to get up in the morning. First 15 minutes can be devoted to such 'me time', and the rest 45 minutes is for working towards your goal.

12. How to increase the value of your property

There're two kinds of changes you can make in your house:
- those that will make your house sell faster in the future,
- those that will make your house sell for a higher price. It all depends on the kind of client you'll be targeting.

Most BBC programmes concerning selling / buying of houses state that it's the **kitchen that sells the house**. The properties for sale or rent draw the attention with the first photo of a nice kitchen, even if the next ones show small rooms. No matter where you live, if you want to quickly sell and increase the value of your property, you should begin with the kitchen. If your home is localised in a good neighbourhood and the price is high, you should invest in quality and design. There're specialist applications that can help with that. I recommend those widely used, with a large number of positive comments: *Design Home, Houzz, Home Design 3D Gold, Magic Plan*.

In more expensive UK cities like London, another means you can use to increase the value of your property by 10% to 15% is adding various types of extensions. Most of them can be done without a planning permission, according to permitted development rights. However, you need a plan from an architect and a final building inspection to confirm that the extension complies with regulations.

Below there're **exemplary works that don't require a planning permission from the local council**. However, sometimes plans from an architect are necessary:
- You can build **a one-storey extension at the back of the house**, but in case of terraced houses it must not extend beyond the rear wall of the original house by more than three metres, and in case of semi-detached houses and detached houses by more than four meters.

- **Small extensions** add around 7% to the value of the property, the bigger ones – even around 11%, according to the information at www.telegraph. co.uk. Make sure however, that the newly created space matches the style of the rest of the house. The size and location of the conservatory will determine whether a planning permission is needed. **A conservatory** costs around £5000–£30,000. Construction valuations depend on many factors, including a surveyor's opinion, the location, the quality of building materials, and others.

- You can **tear down a wall or make a partition** if you live in a normal apartment or house. You only need the planning permission if your property is on the list of buildings with special architectural or historical significance – the so-called listed building.

- You can **replace doors and windows**. However, a permission for this is needed if your property is a listed building or in a conservation area. Make sure you've received a Fensa certificate from the manufacturer when replacing windows. If the windows have been replaced, the buyer's solicitor always asks for this certificate. Sometimes, when the certificate is missing, the buyer gives up the purchase. You also need a permission if you **convert a garage into a room** and put in a window, unless you don't change the structure of the building. If the structure isn't changed, the conversion is qualified as a permitted development, and you only need a change of use permission from a garage to a habitable room(s).

- You can create a **habitable loft**. This counts as a permitted development and doesn't require a separate permission. However, there're some limitations you must bear in mind. In a terraced house the loft space shouldn't exceed 40 square meters. The new room cannot be higher than the highest point of the roof in the existing house. The cost of converting a loft into a room with an *en suite* bathroom is around £20,000–£35,000, depending on the size. If the loft is spacious enough to have two rooms and a bathroom, it would cost about £45,000. It's worth noting that, according to the Nationwide statistics from 2014, a loft room adds 21% to the house value, or around £63,000 if the house is worth more than £300,000. In case of some cities, for example

Liverpool, those statistics aren't relevant, as you can buy a 3-bedroom house even for £50,000.

If your renovation projects are extensive, you need an architect who will prepare drawings for you and apply to the council. The application itself costs £172, plus the architect's fee, which adds up to around £1200–£2000.

🔔 Remember!

Talk to neighbours about your plans of building an extension. Otherwise, if they feel the project will adversely affect the value of their property, they may question it; for example, they may claim that the extension obstructs the light, thereby reducing the value of their property. For this reason, even if your project is fully compliant with applicable law and spatial planning, talk to your neighbours to avoid any misunderstandings.

Don't exaggerate with adding value to the property and the scale of renovation works.

Check the average house prices on your street and align the plan for raising the property value with the information on Zoopla or Rightmove (sold prices section).

There's a risk that you could overinvest and won't see a return on the money you've put in the renovations. Read the example below:

📖 Example

In 2007 I bought an old house that in the Land Registry was registered as a 2-bedroom house. I paid £250,000. It was 2007 and the price was much below its market value. In addition to the major renovation works, I added a dining room, a converted loft with a bathroom, an additional bathroom on the ground floor, and I converted the bathroom on the first floor into another room.

The house was valued at £595,000 in 2017, but in my opinion, it was worth around £650,000, given its size, condition and financial means invested in all the works. The problem was, however, that on this street there were only small two- or three-bedroom houses and only four larger ones, and each appraiser checked the average house value on this street. The prices of the houses sold there were on average £450,000–£500,000 and nobody cared that they were half as big as mine, and that the rent for them was a few hundred pounds lower compared to mine.

Summary of the chapter:

1. Look for a way of increasing the value of your property.
2. Check if you need planning permission.
3. Hire an architect for larger renovation projects.
4. Talk about planned works with your neighbours.
5. Don't exaggerate with increasing value of the property and the scale of renovation works.

Meg and Dan – example

A purchased house is an investment, even if you don't plan to sell it in the near future. It's very likely that the market value of your property will be increasing year by year. This is determined not only by economic factors such as inflation and limited supply, but also by demographic growth, time and changes in the area.

Many economists believe that investing in real estate is one of the best ways to multiply wealth. Especially that, as a homeowner, you can do a lot to increase its market value (I wrote about it in the previous chapter). You don't have to rely on sales trends only and wait the next 10 years for your house to significantly increase its value.

Meg and Dan – example:
The house on sale was in North London. It had three bedrooms, a kitchen, two bathrooms, a garden and a parking space on the street.

The purchase was completed in December 2014. The price of the property amounted to £390,000. The buyers took a mortgage with an interest rate of 2.39%.

December 2014

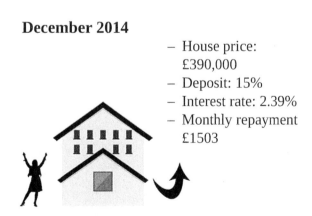

– House price: £390,000
– Deposit: 15%
– Interest rate: 2.39%
– Monthly repayment £1503

Two years after the purchase, the owners remortgaged the house. Thanks to this the costs of their mortgage were reduced.

December 2016

Remortgaging
– Market price: £485,000
– Interest rate: 1.95%
– Monthly repayment: £1230

Market value increases. Interest rate and monthly repayments fall down.

They carried out renovation works which encompassed building an extension and adapting the loft, as well as refurbishing kitchen and bathroom.

Year 2019

– Renovation cost £80,000
– Extension at the back of the house
– Loft adaptation (en suite)
– New kitchen, bathroom, shower room, wall decorating, flooring
– Current value of the house: **£625,000**

Property price from the moment of purchase increased by 60.25%

Summary of the chapter:
1. The property you've bought is an investment because its market value increases over time.
2. You can also increase the value of the purchased property by conducting suitable renovations.

✐ Exercise

Find two people who are your role models. List the characteristics of these people (for example, getting up early, living according to their values, perseverance in pursuing a goal, financial intelligence). Analyse which of these behaviours you can emulate. Go on!

13. Specialists interviews

Architect interview

1. Can you explain all aspects of planning permission?
a. Projects for which permission is required

Generally, planning permission is required for new builds, conversions, extensions, loft conversions of properties, flats and maisonettes, and, in some cases, when there's a change of use. If the property is a listed building or in a conservation area it is most likely you will not have any permitted development rights. There is a handful of conservation areas where this will not apply. The local council planning office would be able to advise you.

b. Projects for which permission is not required

Generally, you have permitted development rights to carry out single-storey rear extensions of up to 3 meters on terrace and semi-detached houses and 4 meters on detached houses. The maximum eaves height from the outside (lowest) ground level must not exceed 3 meters and the maximum ridge height must not exceed 4 meters. If the property is a listed building or in a conservation area it is most likely you will not have any permitted development rights. Flats or maisonettes generally do not have permitted development rights.

c. Most popular extensions and the requirements

The most popular are extensions and the single-storey rear extensions of 3 and 4 meters, but also larger home extensions have become very popular over the last few years. In case of an attached house you can apply for an extension of 3 to 6 meters and for a detached house – 4 to 8 meters. Of course, you would have to follow the guidelines for the height.

Loft conversions have become very popular as well, and in some cases you may be able to get 2 additional bedrooms and a bathroom there.

d. How to prevent things going wrong

Sometimes it is best to consult with a professional Architect or an Architectural Technologist and pay a small fee for a consultation to see what extensions are possible before you proceed with full drawings. You can also look up the properties on your street at the local councils planning application search page to see what has been approved and who has acted as the agent for that property. Some councils planning departments have a duty planning officer that you can book an appointment with for a small charge, and you can show them photos of the outside and get some advice.

e. Should we talk to our neighbours before applying for planning permission?

It is always best to have your neighbour on your side when you decide to extend your property. Sometimes this may not be possible, therefore you should ensure that the person that carries out the drawings for you has a good reputation.

2. Who is a building inspector and what is their role? How can we make sure that we are ready for their inspection? Can we use a private inspector rather than the one suggested by the local council, can you tell us the difference in their service and approach?

The Building Inspector is the person from Building Control of the council or from a Private Building Inspector company that checks the construction drawings including the structural engineers and inspects the construction on site through stages to ensure that the building is being built correctly. You can use a private inspector as longs as the works have not begun yet.

3. What is change of use? What are the examples of the most popular ones and the process of obtaining permission?

Change of use is when you would like to change the property / building to a different use. There are many types of change of use. The most common are when you would like to convert your property to house in multiple occupation (HMO) (C3 to C4), or if you have an office and you would like to convert it to a residential unit (B1a to C3) or even a part of retail unit to create a residential unit. Converting a garage to a habitable room, or adding a habitable basement to your property will also require planning permission, as well as adding a studio flat or converting your property to flats.

4. What permission is needed if we want to have a driveway instead of a front garden?

You will not need planning permission if a new or replacement driveway of any size uses permeable (or porous) surfacing which allows water to drain through, such as gravel, block paving or porous asphalt, or if the rainwater is directed to a lawn or border to drain naturally.

If you require a dropped kerb to create a driveway, you will then have to apply to the council with a dropped kerb application form or in some cases planning permission will be required.

5. In case of the projects where the planning permission is not required, can you tell us, step by step, how the works should be planned?

For extensions and loft conversions where a planning application is not required because it is permitted development, you should still appoint an architect or an architectural technologist to prepare drawings to submit an application called 'Application for a Lawful Development Certificate for a proposed use or development'. This will verify the works and confirm that they comply with permitted development. You will get a certificate. If you ever sell the property, you will have confirmation that your extension complies with the law. You will also need to apply for building regulations approval as per the above noted.

6. What are listed buildings? If the buyers decide to buy one, what challenges will they be facing? Where to apply for permissions and what is the process with most common issues such as replacing the doors or windows, painting the outside etc.

A building is listed when it is of special architectural or historic interest considered to be of national importance and therefore worth protecting. As the term implies, a listed building is actually added to a list: the National Heritage List for England. In case of these buildings, planning permission is required when replacing doors and windows, even for external painting.

7. What are conservation areas? What can and cannot be done in those areas?

A conservation area is an area of special architectural or historic interest, the character or appearance of which it is desirable to preserve or enhance. This means that when a conservation area is designated, the Council has recognised that the area has a special character and identity which is worth protecting. In these areas planning permission is required for extensions, loft conversion, replacing doors and windows, and even for external painting. They generally don't have much permitted development rights.

8. Is permission required for building a greenhouses, sheds or kennels in our gardens?

Generally no. You can build an outbuilding in the rear of the garden as per the following:

a. Outbuildings and other additions must not exceed 50% of the total area of land around the original house. Sheds and all other outbuildings and extensions to the original house must be included when calculating this 50% limit.

b. To be a permitted development, any new building must not itself be separate, self-contained, living accommodation and must not have a microwave antenna.

c. Outbuildings must be single-storey with a maximum eaves height of 2.5 meters and maximum overall height of 4 meters with a dual pitched roof, or 3 meters in any other case.

d. If the outbuilding is within 2 meters of the property boundary the whole building should not exceed 2.5 meters in height.

e. Balconies and verandas are not permitted development. Raised platforms such as decking are permitted development provided they are no higher than 300 mm.

f. Outbuildings are not permitted development forward of the principal elevation of the original house.

9. Please can you explain what Party Wall Act is?

The Party Wall Act prevents building work undertaken by one neighbour from undermining the structural integrity of shared walls or neighbouring properties. It is also designed to avert and resolve potential disputes with neighbours. A party wall award is a legal document, which sets out the rights and responsibilities of the owner instigating the building works and legal owners of the adjacent, or nearby property. Also, a party wall award can provide you the access agreed with the adjoining owner if required for your construction. A party wall award comes with a schedule of condition for the adjoining properties. This will protect the owner carrying out the works from any existing defects the adjoining property has, as well as protecting the adjoining buildings if any defects appear during the construction period.

10. If, after a while, a home owner decide to buy another property and turn their existing home into HMO or two individual flats, what is the step-by-step process, requirements, costs and chances of the application being successful?

To change a residential dwelling into a HMO or convert it into two flats, planning permission is required. Whether or not the application is successful depends on the local situation, the local council's needs and requirements for the area. In your application a good planning statement is always appreciated. You need to include local amenities, transport plan, cycle stores and position of refuse facilities. There are times when, prior to submitting of a planning application, to obtain advice / more information you can make a pre-application.

Contribution by Andreas Georgiou, contact details below:

Andreas Georgiou T/A GIAD

Architect
Georgiou • Interiors • Architectural • Design
p: 020 8200 2331 m: 079 5658 7037
a: Kingsbury House, 468 Church Lane, London
NW9 8UA

Project manager interview

What are the skills that a brilliant project manager should possess?

The main paramount skills:

1. A good all-round communicator. From communicating with the labourer digging the hole in the ground to the architect doing the design – treats everyone the same and communicates as if each is an important part of the process. Including adjoining neighbours.

2. Experience/knowledge. A good project manager I believe should at least be in his mid-30s. A project manager who comes up through the trades understands how to produce a good finish whereas he may not be so good at coordinating design and budget etc. Whereas a project manager who has come through some sort of educational program will be good at budget control and contract issues but not so good at producing a good finish on the project – a healthy combination of the two normally produces a very good project manager.

3. Stand-up thinker and problem solver. Someone who can keep the project going at a pace without having to continually refer to others for information; should be able to solve problems for themselves to a reasonable degree.

4. Lateral thinker, thinking on several levels at once.

5. Keeps a keen eye on the budget. Regularly updates the budget on at least a weekly basis taking on board any variations.

6. Team and worker motivation. Must be able to keep the team going at a pace and get everyone invested in the project.
7. Runs a clean and safe site maintaining health and safety throughout. A clean site is normally an efficient site and also a site where a good workmanship is carried out. It's difficult for workers to respect a project and produce good workmanship when they are not given good working conditions to do this.
8. Sees problems before they occur and takes action to avoid them, for example, in case of a change in the weather for the worse, he/she makes sure that scaffolds are secure down and the building is weathertight.
9. Makes sure that the site is secure as many projects has been finalised with essential items being stolen. I always recommend that CCTV is installed, and this is advertised on the hoarding.

What is project management?

To be able to bring a project to successful completion ideally within budget, specification and program and most importantly to the clients satisfaction. Some people confuse project management with project and administration. These are two entirely different roles, though sometimes they may be combined.

What are the roles and responsibilities involved in such projects?

Some people mix up contract administrators with project managers. The former is basically concerned about controlling contractual liabilities and financial implications. The latter are more about achieving items mentioned above under item 3.

How do you prepare for the commencement of the project?

The key thing is planning. As much information should be decided at the beginning of a project from the kitchen design, bathroom etc. as much as possible, because types of tiles will affect floor finishes. Pick in the ironmongery for the doors, all these should be decided on as early as possible. People have builders quote on projects when none of this information is available at the start and then they wonder why the project goes way over budget.

A good scope of works, specification backed up with priced quantities required enables the project manager /client to keep control of the finances on the project. It is good if the builder prices everything individually as we all change our minds on projects, and we would like to get financial returns when omissions are made. This seldom happens if no price has been agreed for individual items before the project starts. The variations however always appear to get overpriced by the builder trying to build up his profit margin which one can't blame them for.

What are the steps from the beginning of the project to its completion?
1. Draw up a brief for the architect.
2. Approve the architect's drawings in terms of giving you what you require.
3. Go for a pre-consultation with the local planners. You have to pay for it but normally it is well worth it as that will help mitigate any delays in the planning process.
4. Obtain planning permission.
5. Serve party wall notices under the Party Wall etc. Act where required or if required. This is required basically if you are altering the party wall structure between properties or you are excavating within 3 m of your neighbour's property; or you are building on the boundary between properties.
6. Register for building control approval – always better to build from approved Building Control Drawings. It's better that way than on inspections alone which can cause difficulties if building control do not agree with what your builder has done on site. People often mix up planning and building control, but they are two entirely different bodies. The former controls the legality of the project whereas the second is more to do with statutory building regulation compliance, quality etc.
7. Notify the neighbours of when you intend to start. It is not compulsory but if you want to keep the neighbours on your side, it is advisable.
8. Agree the build program with the builder as part of your contract.

What are the necessary licences / documents required before a residential building / construction project is authorised for commencement?

1. Planning or permitted development permission.
2. Building control notification. Be careful when using private building control companies – they must notify the local authority and when they notify the wrong one, this can put the whole project in jeopardy.
3. Engineering calculations and drawings especially if you are doing any such items as installing steel beams, columns etc. to make the building more open-plan.
4. As above party wall notices / schedules of condition of neighbours' property / awards may be needed before you start on site.
5. When large elements such as windows are being installed, you should ask for appropriate certification from the body installing them such as FENSA certification. (I suggest you google this)
6. You should check that your electricians are NIC-qualified and able to issue proper certificates for the wiring.
7. You should check that your plumber/heating installer is gas safe registered and can issue appropriate certificates.
8. You should make sure you get warranties for all major items such as electric garage doors, kitchen appliances etc. Other such items as specialist roof should also have warranties attached. In case the builder is no longer around you can go direct to the subcontractor.

Do you use any project management tools? If so, which of those would you utilise?

Probably the best project management tool for the novice client would be Microsoft project manager which enables a person to sequence activities on site and put a budget to these activities, so as to monitor whether you are on budget or over budget or even – although this is unlikely – under budget!

If it is a refurbishment job, no harm in buying a cheap damp meter to make sure that before decoration commences on-site all the walls are dry. Also, if installing timber floors, to make sure that the right moisture content has been achieved in the floor screeds as this is one of the big common problems found in projects where the works commence without proper checking on finishes.

How do you ensure a safe working environment on a building site?

A clean site is normally a safe site. You should have up posters on the front of the hoarding indicating what safety is required from individuals. Make sure individuals driving items of plant are properly qualified. This is also a big problem area where injuries occur, and it is the owner of the site that is ultimately responsible for this.

How do you monitor project progress within the project schedule and budget?

There is software available to do this such as Microsoft project manager mentioned above.

What do you normally do if you cannot meet the deadlines?

If you cannot meet deadlines as a project manager you must have reasons why the deadline has not been met – was the information not received on time, was there exceptionally inclement weather, did something happen on site beyond your control? There are lots of reasons for this.

What are the factors you would consider while negotiating contracts with clients?

The level of information available, quality of drawings etc. These are probably the most important factors in deciding how the project will proceed.

How do you ensure effective communication amongst all involved in the project?

This is very difficult to answer as it's a very comprehensive process – this involves such things as drawings fully approved. Confirmation of instructions by client must always be in writing.

Client should be advised if any variations are likely, to increase the budget and by how much.

What are some of the challenges you faced?

1. Accidents on site.
2. Sub-contractors going bankrupt, not being able to complete their specific part of the works.
3. Break-ins on site.
4. Burst pipes on site.
5. Wind damage when works are not properly supported at roof level.

Do you manage one or few projects at any one time?

I personally used to manage multiple projects. These days I am more Party wall surveyor and a very little project management as I find it not a very profitable business to carry out unless you are dealing with very well-off clients all the time.

What are the costs involved when hiring project manager?

Most project managers will ask for an 8% fee of the contract value. This is quite high, and it is why most people do not employ a project manager / contract administrator, which is a mistake.

Contribution by Carl O'Boyle, contact details below:

Carl O'Boyle BSc MRICS FCIOB MFPWS

Managing Director
Tayross Associates Ltd.
p: 020 8426 1448 m: 079 7682 0628
a: 2nd Floor Monument House, 215 Marsh Road,
Pinner, Middlesex HA5 5NE

w: www.tayross.com e: carl@tayross.com

14. What will happen if you lose your job

If you lose your job, **you must immediately go to the local Jobcentre Plus office** and register as an unemployed person, even if you have enough savings to make your repayments for the next few months. You don't know how long it'll take you to find a new job, and the Jobcentre Plus will offer financial help and, more importantly, provide documents and instructions on how to repay your mortgage.

🔔 **Remember!**

If you are a homeowner, you might be eligible to get help towards interest payments on your mortgage and loans you have taken out for certain repairs and improvements to your home. This help is called Support for Mortgage Interest (SMI)

From the 6th of April 2018, Support for Mortgage Interest (SMI) is granted in the form of a loan. It must be returned in the event of the borrower's death, or when the property for which the loan was taken will be sold.

SMI cannot help you to pay:

– missed mortgage payments (arrears)
– the amount you borrowed – only the interest on your mortgage
– anything towards insurance policies you have

You can find more information on www.gov.uk

If you fail to find a job for 12 weeks, you can negotiate with the lender, to suspend repayment of the mortgage until you find permanent employment again. The interest will be paid by the government through the Jobcentre. This is a very simple process. The lender doesn't ask any questions and usually doesn't question the length of the break in the loan repayment period. However, this support is available only to residents, so if you haven't yet applied for it, don't delay changing your immigration status.

If you are a UK resident and you lose your job, you shouldn't be worried. The British government is very helpful to first-time buyers. It's in your best interest, as well as the best interest of the lender and the government, that your home isn't repossessed.

Missing repayments

If you stop repaying the mortgage and you don't communicate with the lender (your bank or building society), your home will be repossessed. According to the British law the bank must send you three warning letters and all the necessary information, which usually takes from three to six months. Then your case will be taken to court, which will last up to another six months. So, all in all, the whole process takes around one year.

If, at any given moment during this time, you resume mortgage repayments, the whole process is automatically cancelled, and everything goes back to normal. If you do nothing, the bank will be allowed to repossess your property and then sell it. In this case you lose both your home and your good credit history, so your chances of getting a new mortgage over the course of the next few years are practically non-existent.

If you anticipate that you're unable to keep up with the mortgage repayments then you need to contact the lender at the earliest opportunity. In exceptional circumstances it may be possible to get a 'payment holiday', that will allow you to get a temporary break on repaying your loan which would not affect your credit history. Sometimes lenders can also use other forms of help, but it's very important to notify them about potential problems in advance, and not when you miss the monthly payment.

Summary of the chapter:
1. If you lose your job, you should immediately register with the Jobcentre Plus.
2. The process of if you miss any repayments on the mortgage.

15. How to sell your home?

You should start thinking about selling your house when you buy it. There may be a moment in your life, maybe in six months' time, or maybe in a few years, that the house that you're buying now will become too small or too big, or it will be in a wrong location. Your life situation may require fast sale and it'd be good to prepare for it. Before you make a purchasing decision, think about who your future buyer will be – a first-time buyer, someone looking to relocate, an investor etc.

In some countries it's still very popular to sell properties by displaying an advertisement on a building or publishing information in a local newspaper / on a website. **In the UK almost everyone uses the services of real estate agencies.**

See what **a real estate agent can do for you**. They will:
- arrange free valuation and explain what is the demand for such properties.
- advise you on what could be changed, and what to repair and rearrange so that the property would gain value.
- professionally prepare sales particulars with photos and floor plan.
- advertise your property on their websites, portals and local newspapers.
- send e-mails or letters to potential customers who have registered with their estate agency.
- organise viewings and show your property to potential buyers (preferably, when you are away).
- negotiate the best price on your behalf.
- monitor the sales process by calling you, the buyer, the broker and the solicitor.

This is how you can choose the estate agency that would be best for you:
- Find a list of several estate agencies in your area and check their reviews on Google.

– Look around the neighbourhood and see which estate agency has been trusted by most people (based on the "for sale" signboards in front of the houses); this also indicates that they have a larger marketing budget, and more customers are interested in buying.
– Check if they're members of organisations such as the National Association of Estate Agents. If they are, they need to comply with the rules set by these bodies, which ensures they meet industry standards.
– Choose agencies with enthusiastic professionals; the first indicator for this may be the customer service you receive.

Estate agencies offer **several types of contracts for the sale of properties:**
1. *sole agency* – you hire only one agency and usually pay the lowest rate for their service, for example from 0.75% to 2% of the property sale price.
2. *joint agents* – usually two agencies that share sales commission.
3. *multiple agents* – usually more than two agencies; this arrangement involves a higher commission of around 2–3.5% and access to more customers, but it can also be more chaotic.

Estate agency contracts are usually signed for four to eight weeks. If you decide to go for only one estate agency and there's no sale during this period, you can change it for another agency. It's also worth remembering that you can always negotiate the price or ask for a fixed fee; for example, regardless of the sale price, you pay the agency £3000. I recommend signing a contract based on commission, that is, when the money the agent gets is calculated based on the percentage of the sales price. It'll be an additional incentive for the agent to negotiate a higher price for you.

An agent will prepare valuation of your property. This will be based on prices of similar properties in the area. Comparables include number of bedrooms, condition of the property, and sold prices of properties with the same post code. It's worth asking which pricing strategy a given agency decides on. In my opinion, the most effective one is underselling (the lowest price you can accept), which will prompt more people to want to see your house. The more viewings, the bigger the chance for offers and the opportunity to price at a higher level.

If you decide that your property is worth much more and put it up for sale at a higher price, you risk that there won't be many viewings. As a result, after a few weeks the price will have to be reduced. Such a reduction may scare off customers, especially first-time buyers, who may mistakenly think that there're some problems, for example with getting a loan for this house.

The next step is to decide whether furniture and household appliances will be part of the purchase. The agent will ask about fixtures and fittings.

Fixtures are, for example, wooden floors, built-in wardrobes and in general all the things that are a permanent part of the property and whose removal would worsen its condition (for example there would be holes in the walls).

Fittings mean furniture, paintings and other movables. Some buyers will consider the furniture left behind as a bonus, but others may think it's rubbish. The solicitor who represents you will send you a list of fixture and fittings, and you will need to declare which of these should remain.

The agent will also ask you for the **EPC certificate** (Energy Performance Certificate). An EPC inspection is carried out once every 10 years and shows if your property is energy-efficient. You can check the last time EPC inspection was carried out in your house on www.epcregister.com. The EPC certificate contains information on estimated energy costs over three years and an energy efficiency rating (from A to G) for your property. It also shows potential future savings on hot water, heating and electricity and includes suggestions for changes that you can make to start saving (for example, by insulating floors, walls or the loft).

Since April 2018, **owners of privately rented properties must not sign a new rental contract if their property has an EPC rating below E, i.e. F and G.** A rating of F or G means that the property will have higher operating costs. If you want to improve the building's energy efficiency, you can: replace windows, use energy-saving light bulbs, insulate the roof and walls, replace the boiler, and install energy-efficient radiators (if you have a flat without gas central heating).

Preparing your house for sale

When preparing your house for sale, you should **keep it clean and tidy.** Many people light incense, candles or bake bread to create a home-like atmosphere. Personally, I prefer a fresh fragrance and cleanliness. Artificial odours arouse suspicions as to whether they're used to mask the smell of dampness and mould, a problem with sewage or mice.

If the property is well-kept, without excess furniture, toys, and with made beds, it will appeal to every client, regardless of age. I once viewed an apartment in the evening and it didn't meet half of my criteria, but there was a lighted fireplace in it, and, in the background, I could hear relaxing music. This made me consider buying this property.

Auction is another way of selling your property. You can find local auction houses on Google. There're a lot of them and each has their own terms and conditions, but the buying process is similar. The agent will carry out a valuation of your house, take pictures and prepare information for a catalogue that will be available to anyone interested from two to four weeks before the auction. The cost of this service is around £400, but it depends on the area and the size of the property. It may be between £250 and £1500.

Before the auction prospective buyers can view your property and arrange for an appraisal and valuation. If your house is sold at the auction, the buyer has four weeks to finalise the purchase. The commission for this service is from 2% to 3% of the price achieved at the auction. Sometimes the overall cost is quite high compared to the value of the property being sold, so it's worth investigating it before you decide on this form of sale.

Finalising the sale

The whole process of selling a property is the same as buying. The parties exchange the signed documents during the exchange of contracts, and a few days later there's completion. On this day, usually around noon, your solicitor will confirm that they have received and transferred all the money to your account, in accordance with the document summarising the costs associated with the purchase of real estate minus solicitor's costs and completion statement. Then you hand over the empty property to the new owner in person, or they receive the keys from the agency, depending on previous arrangements. In case of auction sale this process should close in 28 days.

Legal information on cohabitation and property rights

1. I have been living with my partner for some time but we are not married. We now want to separate. Do I have the same rights as married couples on divorce?

Cohabitees are not treated by the law in the same way as married couples irrespective of the time of their cohabitation. The law offers very little protection to cohabitating couples upon separation and they do not have automatic rights to claim against the other upon relationship breakdown. Instead, cohabitants are reliant on the principles of land and trust law to determine any disputes regarding the ownership of the property. The default position is that each individual gets to keep their own property or documented share of any jointly owned property.

The exception to this rule is if the parties were engaged and terminated their agreement to marry; property in which either or both had a beneficial interest during the engagement is subject to the same rules as determine the rights of husbands and wives in equivalent circumstances.

2. Do I have any rights in respect of our family home?

There is no automatic right to family home arising from a cohabiting relationship. There are two distinct scenarios for cohabitees and it depends whether they own the property as co-owners or whether the property is owned by one of them. Many property co-owners do not realise that they can hold a property in more than one way or that the way they own it can also have an impact on their Will.

The co-owners can hold the property in one of two ways, namely: as joint tenants or as tenants in common. The legal estate in a property must be held by co-owners as joint tenants (section 36(2), Law of Property Act 1925 (LPA 1925)); however, the equitable estate may be held as joint tenants or as tenants in common.

If you hold the property as joint tenants, both of you will own the whole of the property. Each joint tenant has an indivisible share in the property and all tenants are equally entitled to the whole property, regardless of their financial contributions. On the death of one co-owner, their interest in the property will automatically pass to the remaining co-owner by way of survivorship and outside the deceased's estate and therefore to the exclusion of any beneficiaries under a Will. If a joint tenant has made a Will that purports to leave their interest in the property to a beneficiary, the disposition would be ineffective.

In contrast, tenants in common own distinct beneficial shares, usually specified at the point of purchase. In the event of a dispute, their respective interest will be determined in accordance with each party's financial contribution. Tenants in common can leave their share in the property in their Will to go to their chosen beneficiaries. In the absence of a Will, their interest in estate will pass under the Rules of Intestacy, upon death.

3. I am not sure whether we own the property as joint tenants or tenants in common. How can I find out?

You can find out what type of ownership you have by checking documents, such as property transfer, deed of trust or by checking proprietorship register whether any restrictions have been added.

4. We own the property as joint tenants. Can I change it?

You can change the way you hold the property with the other co-owner. This is called 'severance of joint tenancy'. The effect of that is that the property will continue to be held by you in your joint names, but instead of owning the property as joint tenants in equal shares, you will own the property as tenants in common in equal shares. This change can be effected by one co-owner without consent of the other or by mutual consent of both parties.

On separation, joint tenants should always consider as to whether to 'sever' the joint tenancy, especially, if they do not wish the remaining co-owner to inherit their share automatically on their death.

There may be various other reasons why the co-owners would choose to change how they own the property. These could be:

- to have his/her larger contribution to the purchase price of the property recognised; or
- to leave their share of the property to another person, either during their lifetime or under a Will; or
- to leave their interest to their children from previous relationships.

5. My partner owns the house, but I have made various contributions to the purchase and upkeep. Do I have any rights to a share in the property?
Cohabitees have no automatic right to a share in the family home if it is held in their partner's sole name. The non-owner will have to demonstrate that they have a beneficial interest in the property and to what extent.

There are two aspects to the ownership of property: the legal tile and the beneficial interest in it. The presumption is that on the basis that 'equity follows the law' the legal owner is also entitled to the entire beneficial interest; however, this is not always the case, and can be rebutted by demonstrating that the legal owner holds the beneficial interest on trust for another.

The trust can be shown to exist by either producing a document in writing that expressly sets out the trust, such as declaration of trust, or by a person requesting the court to infer the existence of trust. It is worth noting that it is not possible to substitute a constructive trust in place of an expressed declaration of trust. Accordingly, one of the first steps in a property dispute between former cohabitees is to establish whether the parties have entered into an expressed declaration of trust.

If there is no expressed declaration as to the ownership of beneficial interest, it may be still possible to establish that the person not on the legal title would nonetheless have the beneficial interest through implied trust or in alternative they may be able to rely on the equitable doctrine of proprietary estoppel.

Implied trust can take form of either resulting or constructive trusts, the distinction between the two is in quantification. Constructive trusts apply to the disputes over beneficial ownership of a shared home in domestic capacity and resulting trusts to disputes over commercial properties. English law classifies flows of money within a family as essentially one of three things: a gift, a loan or a beneficial interest in other property. The differences are largely ones of intention. The presumption that the financial contributions by the non-owner were intended to be recognised as a beneficial interest can be rebutted by evidence that funds were to be a gift, loan or payment for rent. Equity will presume a gift if a donor is under an equitable obligation to make provision for or support another (i.e. parent and child or those engaged to be married). The presumption of advancement, or gift, does not apply to cohabitants. Generally, it will be the intention of the person making the contribution that will be determinative, regardless of whether this intention was communicated to the legal owner.

In brief, in order to succeed in a claim seeking to establish beneficial interest, the claimant would have to demonstrate on evidence that they have either a) made a direct financial contribution to the property, or b) that it was agreed between the parties that he/she would have an interest in the property and there was clear reliance on this to their detriment, or c) there was assurance from the other co-owner that the claimant would be entitled to a share in the property and they relied on this assurance to their detriment. This is a complex area of law that requires specialist legal advice. It can be costly and time consuming to prove that you have rights to the family home unless the claim is supported by evidence demonstrating financial contributions and/or intentions of the parties.

If there is a dispute about the property ownership between cohabitees, the court can make orders to establish who is entitled to occupy the property and decide on the nature and the extent of the ownership, including orders for sale. However, it has no discretion to adjust those interests as in the case of a married couple. If there are children, the court has separate powers of giving the non-owning partner extended rights of occupation so that the accommodation needs are met during the period of children's minority and dependency.

6. How can I protect my position?

There are number of ways to ensure that cohabitees are protected:

Cohabitation agreement – this sets out both partners' intentions in relation to property, finances and how they would support their children if they separate. A cohabitation agreement can be completely bespoke and cover whatever you both agree on.

Declaration of Trust – this sets out how you want to own a property and in what shares, it can also cover what happens if you separate. Whilst each party could be named as a legal owner, entering into a deed of trust can give each party a different share to reflect their personal circumstances. In order for this to be a watertight document there has to be a trust deed. However, if there is no trust deed in existence, the starting presumption is that the property is owned by whoever is on the land registry and if there are two owners and no trust deed in place, the starting point will be that it is owned in equal shares. Anyone proving to the contrary of what is written down has the burden to prove their case.

Will – unless specifically named in a Will, or if a valid Will has not been created, a cohabiting partner does not have an automatic right to inherit or to make a claim on their deceased partner's estate. It is important to make a Will to ensure your property passes in accordance with your wishes. It is especially vital if you have children or family who depend on you financially as a Will is the only way to ensure that your property goes to the people you care about. Unmarried partners may not receive anything from your estate, unless there is a Will in their favour.

Contribution by Barbara Bitis, contact details below:

Barbara Bitis

Solicitor & Collaborative Lawyer
Nockolds Solicitors
p: 020 3892 6800 m: 079 2719 1382
w: www.nockolds.co.uk or www.prawniklondyn.com
e: bbitis@nockolds.co.uk

Summary of the chapter:

1. You should think about the future sale the moment you buy a given property.
2. Use the services offered by estate agents.
3. Prepare the house for sale.
4. Learn about the stages of the sales process.
5. Understand your legal rights on cohabitation and property.

✎ *Exercise*

What do you want to achieve as part of your investment in the real estate, looking after yourself, or taking care of your health? Write down specific actions that will help you achieve your goal and meet the date which you've set. Then think how you need to change and what you need to get to achieve this goal – how much time and money you need, who can support you, what information you lack. Write your answer below.

. . . .

. . . .

. . . .

. . . .

. . . .

. . . .

. . . .

. . . .

. . . .

. . . .

. . . .

16. Investor stories

Property Journey 1: Shane Duff

1. Please can you tell us what was the starting point in your property journey?

The starting point for me was when I was studying at university after retiring from professional sport. I was paying my way through university with a lot more liabilities than incomings. This pattern was not sustainable. I was also concerned that the industry that I was studying (teaching) was not going to pay me the salary that I needed to fulfil the dreams and plans that I had for the future. I had always been interested in property but had never done anything as I was always focused on my sport and being the best I could be. I was already a believer that investing money to generate assets was the best way to increase wealth and help to provide a better life. I took the plunge and paid a significant amount of money for some training/education and then set about buying my first property. The information was heavy and there seemed to be so much. Quite overwhelming at times but also exciting. I was unsure of where to go and how to start but I managed it. I started with a flip project and it worked out well. I made £20,000 but I hadn't paid myself for any of the time I had put into it. I did learn a lot however which I thought was invaluable to me moving forwards. I also learned that this approach of not paying for my time was not a suitable approach to build a sustainable business.

2. Where would you start today if you were new to property investing?

I would start with people who are actively doing it. It is clear that property has ever changing laws and legislation to adhere to. As soon as you read a book or attend some training the information you are hearing/reading is potentially outdated. As soon as you finish reading it all, some aspects may have changed. If I was starting out again I would commit full time for free to people who are active in the industry. I would want to see what goes on all of the time and not just the snippets. I would like to see the groundwork that goes into any property deal – the invisible work as I call it.

I would also seek guidance for any books and self-development seminars to attend. I found that working in industries that are very different to your past requires a lot of change to your own mindset. We are all conditioned by the environment we have chosen or put in and when we change to dramatically we don't often have the internal skills to deal with it. I think to start in property you need to gain knowledge/information and also undertake continuous steps to improve mental capacity.

3. As a property mentor, what is the very first question you ask your clients?
The first question I ask my clients is 'what is your outcome?' or 'why are you investing in property?'. The reason why I ask them this is because I want to know their motivation and if it is clear in their mind. I am aware that people use my services because they want to progress quicker than they had been previously. Clients have witnessed other people's results and can see the successes on the surface but they have not experienced any of the pain that is associated with the route to success. I am also aware that I will be pushing them out of their comfort zone and urging them to work differently in order to achieve different results. With this come resistance and some negative emotions when things don't go how they had envisaged. If clients have a strong reason 'why' then they will have a strong pull in order to keep pushing forwards. The emotional attachment to goals is so important when engaging with activities that are new to the way someone would normally work.

4. Which advice would you give to those who cannot afford to buy a property in the location that they currently live in?
I would advise them to be open to working differently and employ other strategies that work towards their outcomes and goals. People can have set opinions on what

they believe to be true but sometimes isn't actually true. They may not believe they can afford the property but they may be able to if they work differently. It would be important for people to understand why they are investing in property in the first place and really connect with this. Once this is established with a clear vision they can then decide which route or strategy can help get them. If they have the objection of price and location then it would be working out how to overcome this. People generally like to invest in areas close to them because they like the comfort of knowing the area well (this is a generalisation). If price is dictating them away from this location then some time employed into learning another area is an option. There are so many resources available online now to do some due diligence. You can quite comfortably understand a market away from home.

Another option would be to find someone in an area and potentially work with them on it.

Contribution by Shane Duff– Investor & Property Coach

Property Journey 2: Simon Harris

1. Could you share your story of property investment?
So, essentially, I first heard about property investment about 4 years ago. A friend of mine, who I have known for about 25 years (he knew me when I was in the music business), works for a property investment company with an owner based in Canterbury. Basically, they have been buying properties in the centre of Canterbury for the past 6–7 years to build solid portfolio's.

About 5 years ago the company bought one of the properties with a view that they were going to get it developed. They didn't have any planning permission at the time so it took them a couple of years to get everything ready. So, at the time when they bought it, or when this friend of mine knew I was getting into property, he said it was going to take them quite a few years to potentially get it ready. Once I got into the business and got some experience, he suggested we could end up doing it as a joint venture. And so that was the original idea and up until 6 months ago that was very much what was going to happen. I was going to do the development side, they were going to put in the land, I would do the development and we would do this as a joint venture.

But then the owner of the company suddenly got into serious financial difficulties. She needed to get hold of some cash very quickly. They have looked around and decided to sell this particular property as that would give her one and a half million pounds quickly to sort out the financial situation. So, that's essentially how it has happened, how I have ended up buying the whole thing rather than doing a joint venture.

So, it is now what I expect but I have been aware of it for at least 4 years now and it also fits all the criteria that I have been looking for. I like something where there is nothing comparable to it. It is expensive but you can't just go and look at another one down the road because there is nothing else like it at all. It has got all those kinds of features that a development needs, all sorts of unique aspects and all the points that are really important. So, that's really how that has come about.

We are mainly proceeding with the original drawings and plans but they are changing a lot as we go along anyways. As you know, to build brand new houses is actually easier than completing a conversion. The problem with a conversion is that you really never know what's going on with the property. I have engaged a number of specialists, looking at it, but until we actually rip back a lot of the walls we really don't know what we are going to find – ' the unknown'.

There is always a risk, for example, if we got some dry rot or discover another issue, they are all problems that can be resolved. I have got a good team of people now that know how to deal with all of it and probably, reasonably, in a cost-effective way. But then there is an element of being difficult to price. My cost sheet is changing every day. We have now realised we can go up into the roof to make a lot of amendments which will add more value on to it. The cost of doing it isn't particularly high in comparison to what you will get. You should be able to at least double the value of the cost of doing the work. But I also have to adjust lots of other figures to make sure that we make allowances for the unknown aspects and then, once we have pinned that down we will have a better idea.

But we are not going to know a lot of those costs until we are actually in, physically in the building and pulling it apart. So, I am just trying to get to the safety margins which is constantly changing along with the costs. It may have been easy just to knock the building down and build some new flats but I really wanted to do the conversion instead.

2. Why a conversion over new build properties?

It is in the conservation area, but I looked back at the planning history, now the whole site is around about one hectare. The original planning history, when they approached the planners they said, well, actually you have got a hectare of land there, you could build anything up to potentially 30, possibly 40 houses on the whole thing. They said they would like to see a lot of houses going on the whole site but the problem with that would have been around the affordable housing issues and Section 106 which wouldn't have made it viable.

You would have to do it so much cheaper, provide 40 percent of affordable housing and plus a big Section 106 contribution, around a quarter of a million pounds. So, it wouldn't have actually been viable because of the value of affordable housing in the area. There would be no profit in it and you wouldn't be able to build. You would have to sell it for less than it would cost you to build. So, they had to essentially scale it back down because the affordable threshold is 14 or 15 units and over was obviously going to be 14 flats and 7 houses. So, practically, it would have been great to get planning permission to knock the property down and build 25, 30 houses but it never would have worked financially.

3. The number 50 lot, when it comes to affordable housing is it is all over UK or is it different in different parts and can you build as little as few apartments?

It does vary; they can sort of set their own situation. In London they do it two ways, sometimes you get these enormous new developments of say 300 or 400 apartments, especially in the really expensive areas, where there is no affordable housing at all. But they will have paid a massive contribution, millions and millions of pounds in Section 106. So, the site itself is just not like you would be having affordable housing alongside a 3-million pounds flat. That wouldn't work. What they do is they pay the council 5–10 million pounds in a Section 106 contribution or even more in some cases to avoid affordable housing, so they can put that into other infrastructure like schools etc. But it does vary massively and also in London generally there is lots of such developments. Generally, you do have to supply the best part of up to 40, in some cases 50 percent affordable housing. But, of course, in London technically it is easier to do it because the value is so much higher. Whereas in this area we had to provide affordable 3 bedroom houses that a housing association could buy for, to make it affordable to buy them at around £200,000 which is what it will cost for us to buy the land and to build them.

Whereas in London affordable housing is still a bit of an anathema because whilst the properties may end up being 40 percent cheaper than their neighbour which is a private one the values are so much higher in London. The cost of building is more but they are double, triple or sometimes even quadruple the value of affordable housing compared to this area. So, it doesn't make sense but that's the ironic part. We could have ended up having 40 houses on the site but we don't because of the unreasonable government rules on affordable housing.

The government keeps on saying– we need to build so many million houses a year and they don't ever reach more than 20 percent of it because they don't provide the infrastructure to allow that to happen. They tend to blame developers who are essentially land banking these huge swathes of land all over the country. And the reason they are land banking is because they are waiting for the right moment to build otherwise they wouldn't make any decent profit so they need their land values to go up to make it worthwhile.

If the government provided good financial incentives, we wouldn't build on this particular land. If the government said: "we want you to provide lots of affordable housing and we will subsidise certain things in return then that would be a different ball game. The problem that the government have is the cost of providing the houses in the rental sector for the affordable housing market. I don't know how much millions of pounds that the government are paying out on but they could eradicate all of that by putting that money into giving tax breaks or support to the developers to provide them with new housing that people could rent.

4. Taking on another site, possibly church land?

I am really concentrating on trying to get the current project over the line first if I can and then I will look into the church land. It should be really simple to do, it is just a new build, it is very straightforward to build, it is not going to be complicated at all. The church land is potentially an amazing project, it is very exciting. I am slightly wary of the scale of the work that needs to be undertaken on that conversion. I think we have allowed for everything but it has put up the build costs quite a lot. So, with the extra roof space it should work itself out but I could find much less stressful ways of making money and developing new projects, for example new builds and simple refurbishments.

5. How do you deal with the challenges?

I like to tell myself I love a challenge. My HMO is in the centre of Folkestone, it will still work out very well. It was originally going to take about 4 months, we'll probably end up at about 6.5 months, I was hoping it would cost about 170 and we will end up at about 230, 240. We bought the building very cheap and it will still work out very well. But there were so many issues because it was an old commercial building, issues came up that nobody expected to find that caused lots of delays.

One of the issues was no one's fault at all and I thought to myself how I am going to resolve it. But one of the first things that we had to do was, because it was an old commercial building, we had to get a sound test done. You need to check the sound levels between the floors, if you are turning it into a residential building. I knew that they would have effectively failed the levels it needed to be at, so I knew that was going to happen. So, we paid out, it was 400 pounds for the test and they said, it is a fail, but this is where a lot of confusion happened because they then came back and said, if you are converting it into a HMO we believe you have got to create noise insulation between the floors and between the rooms to the same level as if were building new flats, which was insane.

And then what happened was they sent their report to building control, the building control officer then said, well, if that's what they are saying that you need, that's what you are going to have to do. We had pointed out there was no guidelines for this, there was no rules and so the building control officer was hiding behind the people who did the sound testing. So, we then had to get a full report done on what kind of work would be needed to meet those standards. That report cost a thousand pounds. And when their report came back essentially what it meant is that we had to do it because previously we were just going to board over the existing ceilings. What we now had to do was tear down all of the ceilings and we had to put in effectively false ceilings as well as false floors. On the false ceilings we had to put in 2 double board with 15 mil acoustic board, then we had to put rockwool, then on the floor above we had to put 22 millimetre soundboard and then on top of new floorboards. And it was going to cost potentially an extra 25,000 pounds to do that.

So, just getting to that point delayed the project by about a month and a half because there were things that we couldn't do, we had to just do other bits and pieces whilst we were trying to find that out. We figured we didn't have any choice, so we then started to do the work, we tore down all the ceilings and then started to do the work which involved putting the rockwool in and then the double boarding.

Then funny enough actually a lady who I had met on one of the other courses, she is actually a building control officer herself, she works in London and came down to have a look at it and she said, they are wrong, they don't know what they are talking about. So, she contacted the building control officer in Folkestone and said, you have got it all wrong, they don't have to do this, they have to provide standard insulation and fire protection but they don't have to do the noise insulation to the level you are talking about. So, we then suddenly got an email from the building control officer stating that we don't have to do it at all. We had already spent 10,000 or 12,000 pounds getting to that point and it delayed the project by such a long time.

The building control officer informed me, that I could take the other building control to court, stating that I will win and get back not only all the money put into it but also some damages. The problem is I do a lot of projects in Folkston and if I took the Building Control Department to court I may never get planning permission for anything in the area again.

As I said it is delayed by about 2.5 months now and as a result of it and there has been lots of other little bits and pieces which even now we are only about 2 weeks away from finishing it. Even now we are still finding a few problems which we didn't know were there and we are having to repair a lot more extensively. But that's what goes with the territories, that's why it is even more important to buy it well in the first place because the margins are very thin. It is very easy to look at things and think, well, I should be able to get it done for a certain amount. If you get something around 5 percent wrong then you can wipe out all the profit. And there are so many people who get into trouble doing that all the time. So, yeah, that has been a real challenge. And that part has been more complicated than jobs that have been 5 or 6 times bigger.

6. What does the project look like?
It is essentially right in the centre of Folkestone. The building is now split it into two, so it is going to be two 6-bedroom HMOs, over 4 storeys.

7. Do you still manage the house that you were renting by hour – the mental health one?
Well, yeah, it pretty much runs itself; everything is pretty much automated now. So, that one is doing very well. It is located just round the corner from where my HMOs are, in an area called the Bale. It was an old office. If you remember the story, I was going to do an HMO there but changed my mind.

8. How does it work?
Everything is done online. All the counselors book their rooms online. They do their own booking with their own clients of course because that's nothing to do with us. I have got probably 100 counselors that are members of that building; they pay 40 pounds a month in membership fee which gives them anything up to 4 hours and they pay 7 or 8 pounds an hour per hour for every room for all

the time they are going to book after that. So, the booking system is also like an accounting system. When they book it, it puts that booking on their account and at the end of the month all I literally have to do is login and create invoices. So, all the invoices go out automatically to be picked up from the booking system. They go out to all the counselors and then they pay by direct debit. So, whatever the figure is it gets taken out of their account a week after that. It is completely automated. We have cleaners that go in a couple of times a week, there is no receptionist, there is nothing at all. And then 3 or 4 of the counselors themselves, we have got them involved to help run the building, for example if there are things like bulbs that need changing or any little bits of maintenance work and stuff, they essentially just let me know and that's it. But the actual physical business side of it is 95 percent automated.

They all have an entry code into the building, which is specific to them. When a counselor books a room they get given a code to give to the clients for when they turn up which is like a one-off code which means that they can then walk in to the building and then they just go straight to the room. It is a one-off code for that day for them to be able to get into the building.

9. Did you create the software for the booking system?

Well, the booking software originally was something that was made specially for us. I did go fairly high up the tree, I managed to find the people who created the online booking system for Booking.com and I spoke to them. It cost like 4000 pounds, it wasn't hugely expensive. And then I asked them to connect it to accounting software so it is all done automatically, it automatically updates. You can book something on Booking.com and if you have got 4 or 5 other portals it automatically updates that kind of stuff as well. So, I then got another company and we have essentially attached a Sage Accounting system onto that software so it updates Sage and then Sage does the update once a month. So, again it is completely automated. I probably spend 10 minutes a month on it. Just checking some of the basic paperwork and that's really about it.

10. How did you come across this software and what can you do with it – can it be rolled out nationwide?

Well, how it happened originally was just purely an accident. Because there was a problem with the title of the building, there was like a year's delay in being able to buy it so I did a bit of research and found there was this potential market to do and that's how it happened. But then it got me thinking, well, this is an amazing idea.

It could be taken out nationwide and the reality is, I have been spending the last 7 or 8 months doing a huge amount of research about possibly rolling this out on a nationwide basis. When I put it together, it was kind of very much hand to mouth. I was going only by what the counselors were telling me that they wanted and that came together. To roll that out in a much bigger way I mean it was very, time consuming whilst I was doing it but there was nothing else to do with the building.

I had the time to do it but getting sort of initially 50 to 70 counselors signed up to it and whatever else that's a lot of work and a lot of hassle. But I believe there is a way of doing it in a much more formulaic way and what is really interesting, I mean at the moment with the Folkestone property, it is now probably occupied, it is only available at the moment from 8.30 until 6.30 Monday to Friday and it is now booked at about 98 percent capacity. And I have got a waiting list of about 150 counselors who would be able to use it but they can't, there is no room for it. A lot of these counselors all know each other. So, I have actually had calls from people all over the country saying have I got any plans to roll this out.

It is something that I am looking at possibly doing. I am trying to come up with a way this could be rolled out fairly simply. I don't even necessarily want to just take an old house and do it, you need a certain type of a building and where it is, it works perfectly for the old sort of Edwardian, Georgian townhouses. It has got to be in the part of a town which is mainly more commercial, so it is easily accessible for the counselors and their clients. So, there is quite a few things that you have to look for, so that everybody could feel comfortable with it. But there are thousands of those buildings around the country; you could easily do it without any problem at all.

It works best on a commercial property, you got to imagine it is almost like a doctor's surgery, you would have people coming in and out the whole time. But there are lots of these old redundant kind of Edwardian, Georgian buildings which used to be occupied by perhaps one company which would rent the whole building, you know a small accountancy firm. But those are now in the past 10 years a lot of them have moved to under permitted, developmental, residential areas anyway but there are still tens of thousands of those buildings which are not permitted developments. And you wouldn't get residential permission for and there is not really a lot of demand for people who want to rent a whole building of that kind of size, it just doesn't suit the demand.

I have done a lot of research in a lot of towns and cities around the country, there are thousands of those buildings sitting empty or the landlords have perhaps got one floor rented and that's it, they can't give away the other stuff. So, you could buy them really quite cheaply and do this to it. But if you look at what has happened in the serviced office industry and hot desking, there is no reason why this couldn't be done all over the place. But you have to find a particular type of building and location.

11. What is the criteria of the building then – does it have to be sort of in a commercial area to start with and what is the ROI?

The look of the building is very important. You got to remember the people using it, these are mental health practitioners who tend to see their clients in the counselor's home. So, the environment and the look of the building has got to be comfortable for the counselors but also for their clients. So, what I did with that one is, as it was an old sort of Georgian building, the rooms themselves I made them look comfortable almost like a living room, airy, carpets and antique furniture, so everyone feels very relaxed, they don't feel intimidated. It has to feel very homey, not like sort of bland office consulting room, something that feels like you are walking into almost your own home or imagine what it would be like. So, internally it has got to feel right so everybody feels comfortable, externally it has got to be in a kind of an area where number one, it is convenient for people to get to, very importantly but more importantly they feel comfortable in its immediate environment. So, you tend to get this kind of buildings in rows or there are entire streets of them where they are those kinds of Georgian buildings.

So, there is all this commercial area around them but they tend to be office spaces, you might get a few shops there in those rows but you don't get a big industrial, commercial units. It tends to be a quiet area all with similar buildings that have got some residential properties but some commercial properties still being used as office spaces and studios. The immediate environment around it, people have said, has to be accessible and they have to feel comfortable with it. So, it has to be relatively in a normal sized town, it has to be pretty central, you couldn't have it on the outskirts of a town because again getting to it, people don't want to have the hassle.

I have just focused on the mental health practitioners but you have to think about how many professions do you know where there are people who essentially probably work from home, a serviced office may not be practical because they wouldn't want to necessarily use it full time. But then also hot desking is not suitable then because they need their own room. If you could give them access to their own room and ask them to commit to no more than 3 or 4 hours a month there must be tens of thousands of people who would like to be able to go and rent that kind of a room, a professional room in an environment which works for them. So, the mental health practitioner market, there is probably 50,000 mental health practitioners around the UK. I think you can multiply that by 10 when you think of all the people who now work from home but at the moment use a mixture of some serviced office, some hot desking because one doesn't provide all of the answers for them.

It's something you could do right across so many other sectors too as well. And with my building in Folkestone, I have now got enough of a waiting list, I reckon I could do another two. Now, that's just in Folkestone, imagine what's that's like around the country. What you got to look for is towns that have at least, a population of round about 70,000 to 80,000 people within say a 15-mile radius. So, you can take most normal sized towns as probably at least 200 towns I have vet around the country and that doesn't include the cities, I mean London and

Birmingham and Leeds, you could, potentially have room for 30, 40, 50 centers potentially or whatever else. I could just do one or two at a time which is quite attractive in itself or potentially roll it out on a much larger scale.

In terms of doing it on a much larger scale, the first thing I thought about was that this is going to cost a lot of money. I went to speak to some equity companies and they all actually offered to back it if I wanted to roll it out in a very big way which is very encouraging. But what I am actually thinking of doing is probably doing an extra, 2 or 3 centers, but get a group of people to come and help do it initially, so we do it between ourselves and learn all the various aspects. Perhaps get a group of people who would help and number one, fund and also physically put it together and learn through the process.

I now get £140,000 a year in income for that building and my business rates are £13,000 and utilities are very low. And then I have got my mortgage on it but I will actually have the mortgage paid off by the middle of next year. So, the returns are potentially extraordinary but it is a lot of work.

12. Are you allowed to use the profits that you make from the building to pay off the mortgage so you don't have to have it as an income and automatically you don't pay tax?

Yes, at the moment the reality is because the running costs are so low but again remember this is a business, so the mortgage that I am paying I could write off anyway because it is a business. And yes, I have got tax to pay but it is, the beauty of it. The reality is once the mortgage is paid down, one of the first things I could do is turn it into a SIP. So, what I could do is effectively charge myself rent to mitigate some of the profits but put that into a pension. So, it works out extremely well.

Contribution by Simon Harris– Investor

17. Bonus Chapter

Finding the right balance between *Price*, *Yield* & *Growth* can be difficult hence why it is extremely important to understand the reason for your investment as well as calculating all costs to decide if you're going to invest in a particular property. Ensuring that you're up to date with all potential costs that are encountered when investing in a property is vital to its success.

There are multiple ways that a profit can be earned so it's imperative that you get the calculations right before proceeding; you need to beware of gross/net yield, return on investment (ROI), capital growth and property tax in the UK. Regardless of which chosen route of investment that you focus on always ensure that for each property; there is a contingency budget in place to cover the unexpected otherwise you may find yourself in a financial nightmare.

Majority of investors, use the quick and easy method of gross yield to work out if a property is worth investing. This approach is risky as it doesn't go into detail of additional costs that may need to be taken into account such as;
– Agent fees
– Maintenance costs
– Mortgage payments
– Void periods
– Insurance
– Additional charges (leasehold fees or service charge)

All calculations on yield, growth or ROI doesn't factor in tax they are pre-tax. Therefore, if you calculated a ROI as 13.2% bear in mind that it will be less than that after tax. The tax calculated will differ depending on circumstances which can be difficult to calculate beforehand; but do keep in mind this needs to be considered. If unsure you can check GOV.UK website to get an idea of potential tax calculations.

Gross yield – This is the return on a property that the investor is likely to achieve through the rental income divided by its original price. Gross yield gives a generic idea of whether the property is worth investing, because its such an easy way to compare properties most investors use this method however it is not the most helpful as it doesn't take additional costs into consideration. The formula to work out your gross yield are as follows:

Formula for % rental yield

Yearly rental income ÷ Cost of property × 100

📖 **Example**

A 4-bed detached property was bought in a good area for £320,000. For that particular area and size of property the monthly rent on average would be £2000, this will generate a yearly rental income of £24,000. The gross yield for this property will be 7.5%. Straight away this looks like a healthy percentage yield for a property.

Net yield – Is the return on a property that you are likely to achieve through the rental income minus any maintenance and running costs of the property. The 'yield' of a property informs you of an annual return that you may be likely to get on your investment. Net yield is usually calculated by yearly rental income divided by the cost of the property including any additional costs such as maintenance of the property. A good rental yield is anything from 7% and above, anything below that percentage will most likely end up with cashflow issues further down the line. The formula for percentage net yield are as follows:

Formula for % rental yield

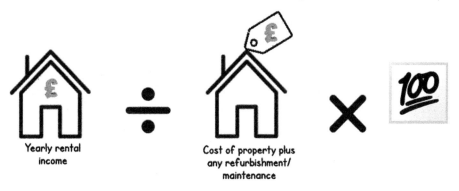

Yearly rental income ÷ Cost of property plus any refurbishment/ maintenance × 100

📖 **Example**

If you had a property that you wanted to let out for £850 per month based on area prices, it will give you a yearly rental income of £10,200. Assuming you bought the property for £130,000 and spent £7,000 in refurbishment and maintenance costs; your rental net yield would be 7.44% giving you a good return on your investment as it is a healthy net yield.

Rental Yield				
Rental value	Cost of property	Maintenance costs	Gross yield	Net yield
£7,200	£150,000	£2,000	4.8%	4.7%
£13,600	£270,000	£4,000	5%	4.9%
£26,200	£465,000	£4,000	5.63%	5.58%

Capital growth – Profit earned if you sell your property for more than you paid for it, it's basically the appreciation in value over time. If you are looking at investing to earn money through capital growth it is worth ensuring that the property is located in an area where house prices tend to rise so that you can generate more money from the property.

It is said that you should also consider the rental yield as well as capital growth even though you may want to make the majority of the profit from capital growth. Consideration of how the property will pay for itself month on month is a 'must'. Growth is calculated by the difference between its current market value and its purchase price at the time the property was acquired. To calculate the capital growth in money and percentage use the formula below:

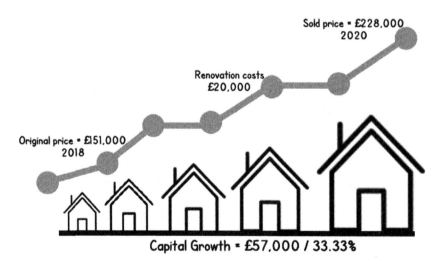

Sold price = £228,000 2020

Renovation costs £20,000

Original price = £151,000 2018

Capital Growth = £57,000 / 33.33%

Current market value - (Original price + Renovation costs) = £ Capital Growth
Capital Growth ÷ (Original price + Renovation costs) = % Growth

A property was bought in a desirable area; within distance of transport, local schools, parks and amenities. Suitable for both families and professionals. The property was bought for £151,000 in 2018. Work was carried out on the property totalling £20,000 putting the total costs of the property to £171,000. In 2020 property prices increased by 39.1% in the area and after a successful sale it sold for £228,000. This generated a healthy capital growth of £57,000 or 33.33% within 2 years.

This is why it is imperative that a lot of research goes into the area that you would like to invest in. Ensuring that not only it may bring a good capital growth as a long-term plan but also the rental yield is sustainable.

ROI – It is said the ROI is the most efficient and effective way to calculate if a property is worth investing in or not. It is the more preferred option than gross yield in understanding the 'ins' and 'out' of the potential investment. The ROI will be similar to the net yield if the property was purchased using your own cash rather than a mortgage because you're inputting full purchase price. With a mortgage there may be fluctuating interest rates which may lower your profit but you will see a better return on investment in the long term. See examples below of both with and without a mortgage. It is better to be a mortgage buyer as there is a greater ROI. Calculate what your ROI would be using the formula as follows:

$$ROI = \left(\frac{Net\ Profit}{Cost\ of\ Investment} \right) \times 100$$

📖 **Example**

Property purchase price of £200,000. For the area the annual costs are;

– Rental income: £9,600

– Maintenance costs: £3,000

– Net profit: £6,600

ROI with mortgage, if cash invested was £50,000 the ROI would be 13.2% which indicates a better return on investment.

ROI without mortgage, would be 3.3% which is not a very good return on investment.

Tax on property – This needs to be factored in when considering investing in a property. Tax is calculated based on the property value, each set within a different band. If the property value falls between two different bands then a portion of each band will have to be paid. It must be paid within 14 days of completion. Due to the coronavirus pandemic in 2020; the tax on property rules changed until March 2021 whereby up to a certain value it is 0% tax. Therefore, seeing an increased number of interests in the property market in particular from investors.

The thresholds are different depending on where you are purchasing the property. For instance, in England and Northern Ireland the threshold has risen from £125,000 to £500,000 for 0% tax. In Scotland the threshold is less than £250,000. However, you must be aware that an additional dwelling supplement (ADS) applies to buy to let investments and second homes. In Wales the current threshold is £250,000 however if you own multiple properties then you may need to pay higher rates.

Property tax rates are a constant change to the property market, the below rates apply up to March 2021. It is worth ensuring that you are fully up to date with the market information through websites such as **www.gov.uk/stamp-duty-land-tax** which will ask you a series of questions about the property; ranging from costs to type of property which will then generate the property tax due. England and Northern Ireland property tax is known as 'Stamp Duty Land Tax' (SDLT). In Scotland it is 'Land and Buildings Transaction Tax' (LBTT) and in

Wales it is known as 'Land Transaction Tax' (LTT). So be sure to familiarise yourself with the correct property tax.

SDLT		
Tax Band	**Normal Rate**	**Additional Property**
Less than £500 k	0%	3%
£500 k to £925 k	5%	8%
£925 k to £1.5 m	10%	13%
More than £1,5 m	12%	15%

The 3% for additional property purchase will only apply on purchases from £40 k to £500 k

LBTT		
Tax Band	**Normal Rate**	**Additional Dwelling (ADS)**
Less than £250 k	0%	4%
£250 k to £325 k	5%	9%
£325 k to £750 k	10%	14%
More than £750 k	12%	16%

The 4% for additional dwelling purchase will only apply on purchases from £40 k to £250 k

LTT			
Tax Band	**Normal Rate**	**Tax band**	**Additional Property**
Less than £250 k	0.0%	Less than £180 k	3.0%
£250 k to £400 k	0.5%	£180 k to £250 k	6.5%
£400 k to £750 k	7.5%	£250 k to £400 k	8.0%
£750 k to £1.5 m	10.0%	£400 k to £750 k	10.5%
More than £1.5 m	12.0%	£750 k to £1.5 m	13.0%
		More than £1.5 m	15.0%

The 3% for additional property purchase will only apply on purchases from £40 k to £180 k

The rate of tax not only depends on the type of property that you are buying but also the type of buyer you are and whether you are a resident or not. There are useful calculation websites that will take into consideration all of these elements; with one of the useful websites to do this is www.stampdutycalculator.org.uk

Summary of the chapter:

1. Understand the reason for your investment and the ways in which money can be made.
2. Calculate all costs before making a decision on an investment.
3. Ensure that you have a contingency budget.
4. Research as much as possible so that you know the area.

📖 Example

Understand the different ways to make a profit on an investment. List the reasons for your investment and which route you would like to proceed with. Analyse the benefits of the potential investment but be sure to understand the risks also. You want to ensure that the property is financially worth it. Grab the opportunity!

Printed in Great Britain
by Amazon

79217815R00086